# Islamic Transformation: Building a Better You, One Islamic Habit at a Time

Nurturing Personal Growth Through Small, Consistent Changes

Aisha Othman, Esquire

To my beloved children

May this book be a gentle guide for you as you navigate the path of life. Every small action, every consistent habit, can transform not just who you are but who you aspire to be in the sight of Allah. I dedicate these words to your growth, struggles, and victories. May you find strength in faith, peace in small efforts, and purpose in every moment of transformation. You are my inspiration, light, and constant reminder that positive change begins within us, one habit at a time.

With all my love,

Mom

The Prophet Muhammad (peace and blessings be upon him) emphasized: "The most beloved deeds to Allah are those that are consistent, even if they are small."

[Sahih Bukhari]

Copyright © 2024 by Aisha Othman

Email: darannoor1@gmail.com

All rights reserved. No part of this book may be reproduced, distributed, or transmitted in any form or by any means, including photocopying, recording, or other electronic or mechanical methods, without the prior written permission of the publisher or author, except in the case of brief quotations embodied in critical reviews and certain other non-commercial uses permitted by U.S. copyright law.

This publication is intended to provide accurate and authoritative information regarding the subject matter presented. It is distributed with the understanding that neither the author nor the publisher is engaged in providing legal, financial, accounting, or other professional services. While every effort has been made to ensure the accuracy of the content, the author and publisher make no representations or warranties regarding the completeness or accuracy of the information contained within. The advice and strategies outlined in this book may not be applicable to your individual situation. It is recommended that you seek professional guidance as needed.

Neither the author nor the publisher shall be liable for any loss of profit, personal or business damages, or any other form of commercial loss, including special, incidental, or consequential damages, arising from the use or reliance upon the information contained in this book.

First edition, 2024

# Contents

| | |
|---|---|
| Preface | X |
| Introduction | 1 |
| 1. The Spiritual Awakening | 3 |
|     1.1 Understanding the Concept of Tawheed (Monotheism) | |
|     1.2 The Impact of Shahadah (Declaration of Faith) | |
|     1.3 The Spiritual Shift That Accompanies the Acceptance of This Testimony | |
|     1.4 Experiencing a Spiritual Rebirth | |
| 2. Finding Purpose and Meaning | 13 |
|     2.1 Islamic Perspective on the Purpose of Life | |
|     2.2 Aligning Personal Goals with Divine Purpose | |
|     2.3 Living a Purpose-Driven Life | |
| 3. Developing a Strong Moral Compass | 18 |
|     3.1 Foundations of Islamic Ethics and Morality | |
|     3.2 Cultivating Honesty, Integrity, and Trustworthiness | |
|     3.3 Practicing Patience, Gratitude, and Humility | |
| 4. Avoiding Sins | 23 |
|     4.1 The Advice of 'Umar ibn Al-Khattab to Sa'd ibn Abi Waqqas | |
|     4.2 Lessons From the Advice | |
|     4.3 How to Avoid Sins | |
| 5. Consistency in Islam | 37 |
|     5.1 Consistency in Worship and Acts of Devotion | |

5.2 Consistency in Good Character and Moral Conduct
   5.3 Consistency in Seeking Knowledge and Personal Growth
   5.4 Consistency in Social Responsibilities and Community Engagement
   5.5 Consistency in Patience and Perseverance
   5.6 The Role of Consistency in Building Faith (Iman)
   5.7 Practical Ways to Cultivate Consistency in Islam

6. Forming Good Habits                                              42
   6.1 The Importance of Intentions in Habit Formation
   6.2 Consistency and Persistence in Developing Good Habits
   6.3 Encouragement to Start Small and Build Gradually
   6.4 The Role of Environment and Community in Habit Formation
   6.5 Self-Discipline and Control Over Desires
   6.6 Making Habits Attractive and Satisfying
   6.7 Reducing Friction to Make Good Habits Easier
   6.8 Leveraging Accountability and Community Support
   6.9 Seeking Forgiveness and Renewing Intentions
   6.10 Reward and Motivation in Habit Formation
   6.11 Utilizing Daily Rituals for Habit Building
   6.12 Habit of Gratitude and Positive Thinking
   6.13 Accountability and Self-Monitoring

7. Building a Positive Mindset and Inner Peace                      51
   7.1 The Power of Positive Thinking in Islam
   7.2 Achieving Inner Peace Through Remembrance of Allah (Dhikr)
   7.3 Overcoming Negative Emotions and Thoughts

8. The Role of Worship in Personal Growth                           56
   8.1 Prioritizing Worship of Allah Most High
   8.2 Daily Rituals and Their Transformative Power
   8.3 The Transformative Experience of Ramadan and Fasting (Sawm)
   8.4 The Impact of Charity on the Soul

       8.5 Hajj (Pilgrimage) and Its Life-Changing Impact

9. Social Transformation Through Islamic Values                 70
       9.1 The Role of Family and Community in Personal Growth
       9.2 Islamic Principles of Social Justice and Equality
       9.3 Promoting a Culture of Compassion and Kindness

Mid Review Request Page                                           75

10. Financial Ethics and Prosperity in Islam                  76
       10.1 The Islamic Perspective on Wealth and Prosperity
       10.2 Implementing Fair Trade and Avoiding Riba (Usury)
       10.3 The Role of Zakat and Sadaqah in Wealth Redistribution

11. Health, Wellness, and Islamic Practices                    82
       11.1 The Importance of Physical Health in Islam
       11.2 Mental Health and Emotional Well-Being in Islam
       11.3 The Healing Power of Faith and Spiritual Practices

12. The Power of Kindness to Parents in Islamic Personal Growth    87
       12.1 The Pleasure of Parents is the Pleasure of Allah
       12.2 Developing Empathy and Emotional Intelligence Through Being Dutiful to Parents
       12.3 Dutiful to Parents Teaches Consistency in Action
       12.4 Kindness to Parents Reflects Relationship with Allah
       12.5 Understanding Why Some Children are Not Dutiful Kind to Their Parents

13. Relationships and Community Building                      95
       13.1 Building Strong Marriages and Family Bonds
       13.2 Strengthening Community Ties and Building a Supportive Ummah
       13.3 Conflict Resolution and Promoting Social Harmony

14. Overcoming Challenges and Striving for Excellence          100
       14.1 The Islamic Perspective on Challenges and Trials

14.2 Developing Resilience and Perseverance
14.3 Striving for Excellence (Ihsan) in All Aspects of Life
14.4 Navigating Modern Challenges with Faith and Integrity

15. Preparing for the Hereafter — 107
    15.1 Belief in the Afterlife
    15.2 Prioritizing the Hereafter
    15.3 Living with a Higher Purpose
    15.4 Continuous Self-Reflection and Repentance
    15.5 Aligning Worldly Actions with Eternal Goals
    15.6 The Role of Good Deeds and Acts of Worship

16. How Islam Transformed the Early Generation of Muslims — 112
    16.1 Spiritual Awakening and Monotheism
    16.2 Moral and Ethical Transformation
    16.3 Social Justice and Community Building
    16.4 Unity and Brotherhood
    16.5 Intellectual and Educational Transformation
    16.6 Political and Economic Reformation
    16.7 Endurance and Resilience in Faith

17. The Islamic Golden Age and Lessons — 117
    17.1 The House of Wisdom and the Translation Movement
    17.2 Advancements in Science and Medicine
    Mathematics
    17.3 Contributions to Philosophy and Theology
    17.4 Literature and the Arts
    17.5 Impact on the Western World and Legacy
    17.6 Lessons from the Islamic Golden Age

18. Islamic Andalusian Age and Lessons from the Fall of Andalus — 124
    18.1 The Rise of Al-Andalus
    18.2 Cultural and Intellectual Achievements
    18.3 Architectural Marvels

18.4 Religious Tolerance and Coexistence
18.5 The Decline of Al-Andalus
18.6 Legacy and Impact of the Andalusian Age
18.7 Lessons from Al Andalus

| | |
|---|---|
| Conclusion | 131 |
| End Book Review Request Page | 136 |
| References | 137 |

# Preface

In the Name of Allah, the Most Merciful, the Most Compassionate. All praise is due to Allah, Lord of the Worlds. We give thanks to Him for guiding us to Islam. Peace and blessings be upon our beloved Prophet Muhammad, the exemplar of righteousness, as well as upon his family and companions, those who followed them, and all the righteous.

I ask Allah Most High to make this work purely for His sake and to reward, out of His generosity, those who have taught me, those who read this book, and those who take benefit from it and pass it along. May Allah bless this effort, and may it serve as a source of inspiration for all who seek self-improvement through the divine guidance of Islam.

All praise is due to Allah, Lord of the Worlds. If this work is successful, it is due to Allah's generosity; if there are mistakes, they are from my shortcomings. I ask Allah to guide and protect me and my family, for He supports those who rely on Him. I seek Allah's forgiveness for my shortcomings and pray for His blessings of well-being and success in this world and the next.

Aisha Othman, Esquire
Rabi'ul Awwal 27, 1446 / October 1, 2024
California, USA
www,darannoor.com

# Introduction

In today's fast-paced world, many people, regardless of their background or beliefs, grapple with a sense of emptiness and disconnection. Despite technological advancements and modern conveniences, there's a growing awareness that material success alone does not bring fulfillment. Humans, universally, yearn for deeper meaning, purpose, and a sense of connection to something greater than ourselves.

Islam offers a comprehensive framework for personal transformation that addresses every aspect of life—spiritual, emotional, intellectual, social, and physical. This book explores how embracing Islamic principles can transform your life, providing clarity, direction, and a profound sense of peace.

Islam is not merely a religion but a complete way of life. It guides how to achieve success in this world and the Hereafter, emphasizing balance, justice, compassion, and resilience. These principles can be applied in your daily life, from how you conduct business to how you treat your family and friends. Through its teachings, one can experience a profound transformation, leading to a more meaningful, fulfilling life.

This book is an invitation to explore how Islam can transform your life from within, instilling a sense of purpose and guiding you toward personal excellence. It empowers you to reach your full potential and fosters a deeper connection with your Creator and fellow human beings, leaving you feeling spiritually fulfilled and deeply connected.

In an ever-evolving world filled with distractions, pressures, and constant demands for our time, the pursuit of personal growth can seem overwhelming. But within the beautiful framework of Islam, we find a profound truth: true transformation begins with small, consistent steps. It is not in grand gestures or instant changes, but in the regular, mindful habits that we cultivate over time, that we build lasting character and closeness to Allah.

In "Islamic Transformation: Building a Better You, One Islamic Habit at a Time", we explore the path to personal growth through the lens of Islamic teachings and values. This book is not about radical changes or lofty ambitions; rather, it is a journey of nurturing the soul through the timeless wisdom of small, consistent actions—actions rooted in faith, supported by the Qur'an and Sunnah, and designed to foster a deeper connection with our Creator.

We will explore how seemingly simple daily habits, such as regular prayer, dhikr (remembrance of Allah), mindfulness in our interactions, and gratitude, can transform us. With each chapter, you will discover practical ways to incorporate these habits into your daily routine, and you'll see how Islam's comprehensive guidance encourages balance, mercy, and personal accountability.

Islam teaches us that Allah does not expect perfection, but effort. The Prophet Muhammad (peace and blessings be upon him) said, "The most beloved of deeds to Allah are those that are consistent, even if they are small" (Sahih Bukhari). This guiding principle is the foundation of the journey you are about to embark on. Together, we will explore how small, sustainable changes in your daily life can create a ripple effect of transformation—shaping your character, strengthening your faith, and nurturing a meaningful relationship with Allah.

May this journey inspire you to take those steps, one habit at a time, toward becoming the best version of yourself in the eyes of your Creator.

# Chapter One

# The Spiritual Awakening

Spiritual awakening in Islam marks the beginning of a transformative journey that aligns a person's life with divine guidance and purpose. It is the process of turning inward, recognizing the need for a higher connection, and understanding one's place in the universe. This awakening can be triggered by various life events, such as personal crises, moments of reflection, or exposure to Islamic teachings. In this chapter, we will explore how Islam facilitates spiritual awakening and the transformative impact it can have on an individual's life.

## 1.1 Understanding the Concept of Tawheed (Monotheism)

At the core of the Islamic faith is the concept of Tawheed, or the oneness of Allah (God). Tawheed is the fundamental principle that defines a Muslim's relationship with the Creator and is the foundation upon which all other beliefs and practices are built.

### Definition and Significance of Tawheed

Tawheed is the belief in the absolute Oneness of Allah. It encompasses the idea that Allah is the sole creator, sustainer, and ruler of the universe. This concept is the foundation of Islamic spirituality, emphasizing that no deity is worthy of worship except Allah. Tawheed shapes a Muslim's worldview, instilling a sense of purpose and direction in life.

### How Tawheed Provides a Foundation for Inner Peace and Focus

Recognizing the Oneness of Allah leads to a profound sense of inner peace and focus. When a person believes in Tawheed, they acknowledge that all events—good or bad—are part of Allah's divine plan. This belief fosters patience, resilience, and contentment, as one trusts that Allah's wisdom is beyond human understanding. By submitting to the will of Allah, a Muslim finds peace in knowing that they are part of a greater purpose.

### Moving from Polytheism or Atheism to a Belief in One God: A Transformative Experience

For many, accepting the Oneness of Allah is a transformative experience that shifts their entire perspective on life. The transition from polytheism or atheism to monotheism involves letting go of past beliefs and practices and embracing a new, unified understanding of existence. This shift often brings a sense of clarity and fulfillment as individuals find themselves aligned with a clear and singular purpose: to worship and serve Allah.

## 1.2 The Impact of Shahadah (Declaration of Faith)

The Shahadah, or declaration of faith, is the first and most fundamental of the Five Pillars of Islam. It is a simple yet profound statement that encapsulates the essence of Islamic belief: "Ashhadu an la ilaha illallah, wa ashhadu anna Muhammadur Rasulullah" ("I bear witness that there is no god but Allah, and I bear witness that Muhammad is the Messenger of Allah").

### What It Means to Bear Witness That There Is No God but Allah, and Muhammad Is His Messenger

The Shahadah is far more than a simple verbal affirmation; it represents a profound commitment to a transformative way of life. By stating, "There is no god but Allah," a person pledges to reject all forms of idolatry and false worship, embracing the belief that only Allah, the One and Only, is worthy of worship.

This commitment is not just a denial of polytheism but a dedication to Tawheed, the Oneness of God, which is the core of Islamic belief. It involves aligning one's actions, thoughts, and intentions with the understanding that Allah alone is the Creator, Sustainer, and Judge of all that exists.

Acknowledging that "Muhammad is His Messenger" signifies accepting the teachings and practices of the Prophet Muhammad (peace and blessings be upon him) as the perfect model for human conduct. This part of the Shahada recognizes the Prophet (peace and blessings be upon him) as the final messenger in a long line of prophets sent by Allah to guide humanity. It commits the believer to follow the Quran, the revealed word of Allah, and the Sunnah, the Prophet's traditions, as the primary sources of guidance in all aspects of life—spiritual, moral, social, and legal.

Bearing witness to these truths means undertaking a comprehensive and ongoing transformation. It involves continually learning about and applying Islamic teachings to everyday life, from personal conduct and worship to social justice and community relations. It requires a believer to adhere to the Five Pillars of Islam, which include daily prayers, fasting during Ramadan, giving to charity, and performing the Hajj pilgrimage if able. The Shahada also fosters a sense of belonging to a global Muslim community (Ummah), transcending race, nationality, and social status.

Additionally, the Shahadah is a constant reminder of the believer's purpose in life: to worship Allah alone and live according to His divine guidance. This declaration shapes a Muslim's identity, influences their decisions, and directs their actions. It is a call to strive for personal and spiritual growth, develop humility, patience, and compassion, and seek Allah's pleasure in all matters.

Ultimately, the Shahadah is a comprehensive commitment to embodying Islamic values and principles in every facet of life. It is a pledge to strive for righteousness, seek forgiveness for one's shortcomings, and maintain a continuous, conscious awareness of Allah in all actions, thereby living a life that reflects true submission to the Creator.

## 1.3 The Spiritual Shift That Accompanies the Acceptance of This Testimony

The acceptance of the Shahada often marks a spiritual rebirth. For many converts to Islam, this moment is characterized by a deep sense of peace, clarity, and purpose. It is the beginning of a journey towards understanding, practicing, and internalizing the teachings of Islam. This spiritual shift is transformative, as it reorients one's priorities, values, and actions towards seeking Allah's pleasure.

### Stories of Reverts and How the Shahada Transformed Their Lives

Numerous stories of reverts (converts to Islam) illustrate the profound impact the Shahadah can have on an individual's life. Many reverts describe feelings of inner turmoil, confusion, or a lack of direction before discovering Islam. After taking the Shahada, they often speak of a newfound sense of peace, purpose, and fulfillment. These personal testimonies highlight the transformative power of embracing Tawheed and the Prophetic guidance.

### Story of Conversion of Muhammad Ali

Muhammad Ali, born Cassius Clay in 1942, was not only a boxing legend but also a powerful symbol of spiritual transformation. Raised in a racially segregated America, Ali gained fame after winning an Olympic gold medal and, in 1964, the heavyweight championship. Around this time, he encountered the Nation of Islam (NOI), drawn to its message of Black empowerment and resistance to oppression. Under the influence of Malcolm X, Ali embraced Islam and changed his name, rejecting his "slave name" and claiming a new identity rooted in faith and dignity.

His conversion marked a deeper spiritual journey. In 1967, Ali famously refused military service during the Vietnam War due to his religious beliefs, leading to a ban from boxing and significant backlash. Despite the cost, he remained committed to his principles, saying, "I'm free to be who I want to be."

In the 1970s, Ali transitioned from the NOI to Sunni Islam, especially after performing Hajj in 1972, where he experienced the universal brotherhood of the Muslim Ummah. His embrace of mainstream Islam emphasized peace, justice, and equality.

Throughout his life, Ali's faith guided his activism for racial justice and humanitarian causes. His legacy as "The Greatest" extended beyond the ring, demonstrating that true greatness comes from the courage to stand by one's beliefs and values.

**Story of Conversion of Aisha and AbulHaqq Bewley**

Aisha Bewley, a notable translator of classical Islamic texts, and her husband, Abdalhaqq Bewley, converted to Islam during the 1960s, a time of significant social upheaval and a widespread search for deeper spiritual meaning. They were originally from the United Kingdom, and their conversion journey began as they explored different spiritual paths, trying to make sense of the world and their place in it.

Both Aisha and Abdalhaqq were drawn to the teachings of Islam after interacting with Muslim communities and reading the Qur'an. The clarity and universality of the Qur'an's message struck them profoundly. For Aisha, the spiritual aspects of Islam, its emphasis on direct connection with the Divine, and its comprehensive guidance on all aspects of life resonated deeply. The couple found in Islam a way of life that aligned with their quest for truth and authenticity, and they formally embraced the faith in the late 1960s.

After their conversion, they embarked on a journey to learn more about their newfound religion. Aisha Bewley devoted herself to studying Arabic and the traditional sciences of Islam, as she was eager to access the Qur'an and classical Islamic texts in their original language. Her dedication led to her becoming one of the most respected translators of key Islamic works into English, including the Qur'an, the Muwatta of Imam Malik, and many classical texts on Sufism and theology. Abdalhaqq Bewley also focused on Islamic knowledge, dedicating his life to teaching, guiding others, and spreading Islamic teachings in accessible ways.

Their transformation was not just about acquiring knowledge but also about embodying Islamic values in their everyday lives. They moved to various

Muslim-majority countries, such as Morocco, to immerse themselves in Muslim culture and gain a deeper understanding of Islamic spirituality. They also became part of the Murabitun community, a movement focused on reviving traditional Islamic practices and the economic systems based on zakat and mutual support.

Aisha and Abdalhaqq Bewley became pioneers in translating essential Islamic works into English, making them accessible to a broader audience, particularly in the West. Their translations helped bridge the gap for new Muslims and seekers of knowledge who did not have access to the Arabic language. Through their works, they have significantly impacted the understanding of Islam in the English-speaking world, particularly regarding Sufism and the Maliki school of jurisprudence.

Their journey of conversion and transformation is marked by their dedication to making Islamic knowledge accessible, their commitment to authentic Islamic practice, and their efforts to connect Western Muslims to the depth and richness of their faith. The Bewleys have contributed to the understanding of Islam, inspiring countless individuals through their scholarship, sincerity, and lifelong dedication to the deen.

**Story of Conversion of Shaykh Nuh Keller**

Shaykh Nuh Ha Mim Keller, born in the United States in 1954, converted to Islam in 1977 after exploring various spiritual traditions during college. Dissatisfied with Western philosophy and Christian teachings, he found the Qur'an's emphasis on the Oneness of God deeply meaningful. After embracing Islam, he traveled to the Middle East, studying under renowned scholars in Jordan, Syria, and Egypt, focusing on Islamic jurisprudence and Sufism.

Shaykh Nuh is best known for his translation of "Reliance of the Traveller," a Shafi'i manual of Islamic law, and for his teachings within the Shadhili Sufi order. He emphasizes inner spiritual development, adherence to Sharia, and integrating outward practices with inward sincerity. Residing in Jordan, he leads a community focused on spirituality, humility, and character refinement, embodying his transformative journey to Islam.

## Story of Conversion of Shaykh Yahya Rhodus

Shaykh Yahya Rhodus grew up in Kansas, USA, and converted to Islam in 1996 at 19. He was inspired by the discipline, humility, and pure monotheism he saw in his Muslim friends. After converting, Shaykh Yahya felt a strong urge to seek traditional Islamic knowledge, leading him to study in places like Mauritania, Yemen, and Syria under renowned scholars like Habib Umar bin Hafiz.

Studying in these traditional Islamic settings, particularly under the guidance of Habib Umar, transformed Shaykh Yahya's understanding of Islam. His conversion brought him a deep sense of inner peace and purpose, leading him to embrace the values of service, humility, and spiritual growth that have become the core of his teachings.

Shaykh Yahya has often spoken about how the practice of Islamic spirituality (Tasawwuf) and the emphasis on good character were particularly impactful in his development as a Muslim. He found profound meaning in the idea that true spirituality is connected to serving others, purifying the heart, and embodying the Prophetic character.

Today, Shaykh Yahya Rhodus is widely known for his work in spreading traditional Islamic knowledge in the West, focusing on spirituality, ethics, and the teachings of the Prophet Muhammad (peace be upon him). His journey from a seeker in Kansas to a respected Islamic scholar is a testimony to the transformative power of faith and the importance of consistent learning and self-development in Islam.

## Story of Conversion of Yusuf Islam (Cat Stevens)

Yusuf Islam, formerly known as Cat Stevens, was a famous musician in the 1960s and 70s with hits like "Wild World." Despite his success, he felt unfulfilled. In 1976, after a near-death experience while swimming off Malibu, he called out to God and promised to dedicate his life if saved. Soon after, his brother gave him a Quran, and its teachings resonated deeply with him.

In 1977, Stevens embraced Islam, changing his name to Yusuf Islam. He left the music industry for almost two decades to focus on Islamic education and charity, founding several schools and organizations, such as Small Kindness, which supported orphans and refugees.

Yusuf returned to music in the early 2000s, using it to spread messages of peace and spirituality. Islam brought him inner peace, redirected his life towards philanthropy, and transformed his music into a tool for promoting unity and understanding. His journey from a pop star to a spiritual humanitarian remains an inspiration.

## Story of Conversion of Shaykh Sulayman Van Ael

Shaykh Sulayman Van Ael, originally from Belgium, has an inspiring journey of conversion and transformation. Born in a non-religious environment, Shaykh Sulayman grew up without strong spiritual guidance, often questioning the purpose and meaning of life. He experimented with different worldviews and philosophies, but none gave him a sense of fulfillment.

His turning point came as a young adult when he began interacting with Muslims. Their warmth, sincerity, and sense of purpose intrigued him, prompting deeper exploration into Islam. He read the Qur'an and was particularly struck by its clarity, logic, and emphasis on direct communication with the Creator. The concept of Tawhid, the Oneness of God, resonated with him deeply, leading him to convert to Islam in his early twenties.

After his conversion, Shaykh Sulayman embarked on a journey to gain a deep understanding of the faith. He traveled to different parts of the Muslim world, including Morocco, Jordan, and Mauritania, where he studied traditional Islamic sciences under well-known scholars. He learned Arabic and studied Qur'anic exegesis (Tafsir), jurisprudence (Fiqh), and the inward dimensions of faith through Sufism.

His transformation was not limited to gaining knowledge—it was also about embodying the character and values of a practicing Muslim. Shaykh Sulayman became known for his focus on the spiritual aspects of Islam, promoting a balanced approach that combined outward practice with inner purification.

Today, Shaykh Sulayman Van Ael is a respected scholar, teacher, and community leader. He focuses on making Islamic teachings accessible to Western audiences, drawing on his experience as a European convert. He is dedicated to fostering a deeper understanding of Islam's spiritual and moral dimensions, emphasizing the need for Muslims to live as positive contributors to society. His journey is a testament to the transformative power of faith, knowledge, and sincere practice.

## 1.4 Experiencing a Spiritual Rebirth

Spiritual rebirth in Islam is not a one-time event but a continuous process of renewal, repentance, and self-improvement. Islam encourages believers to constantly seek forgiveness and strive for spiritual growth, recognizing that every day is an opportunity for transformation.

### Understanding the Concept of Spiritual Rebirth in Islam

In Islam, spiritual rebirth refers to the continuous renewal of faith and commitment to Allah. This process is marked by sincere repentance (Tawbah), seeking forgiveness for past sins, and making a conscious effort to improve one's character and deeds. It is an ongoing journey of self-purification and striving towards spiritual excellence.

### How to Cultivate a Sense of Spiritual Renewal Daily

Cultivating a sense of spiritual renewal involves regular self-reflection (Muhasabah), engaging in Dhikr (remembrance of Allah), and consistently seeking knowledge and improvement. By setting aside time each day for prayer, reflection, and Quranic study, Muslims can maintain a strong connection with Allah and continually renew their commitment to their faith.

### Examples of Personal Transformations Through Spiritual Practices

Many Muslims have experienced profound personal transformations through consistent spiritual practices. These practices, such as regular Salah, fasting, and charity, help cultivate a deeper connection with Allah, instill discipline, and promote positive character development. Personal stories of transformation illustrate the power of these practices to change lives, leading to greater fulfillment, purpose, and spiritual growth.

The spiritual awakening in Islam is a powerful and transformative experience that can reshape every aspect of a person's life. By embracing the core principles of Tawheed, committing to the Shahadah, and engaging in spiritual practices, individuals can cultivate a profound connection with Allah and embark on a journey of continuous growth and self-improvement. This chapter has explored the transformative potential of Islamic spirituality and laid the foundation for further discussion on how Islam can lead to holistic transformation in all areas of life.

We will continue to explore other aspects of transformation through Islam, including finding purpose, developing a strong moral compass, building a positive mindset, and achieving personal and social growth. Each chapter will delve deeper into how Islamic teachings can bring about profound and lasting change in one's life.

# Chapter Two
# Finding Purpose and Meaning

Finding purpose and meaning is a fundamental aspect of the human experience. Many people spend their lives searching for what gives them a sense of fulfillment, direction, and peace. In Islam, the purpose of life is clearly defined and is rooted in worshiping Allah and living according to His guidance. This chapter will explore how Islam provides a comprehensive framework for understanding life's purpose, aligning personal goals with divine purpose, and living a life of intentionality and fulfillment.

## 2.1 Islamic Perspective on the Purpose of Life

Islam offers a clear and profound understanding of the purpose of life, which is deeply rooted in the concept of worship and servitude to Allah. This purpose transcends worldly achievements and is centered on seeking Allah's pleasure and preparing for the Hereafter.

### Quranic Verses and Hadith that Define the Purpose of Life

The Quran and Hadith provide explicit guidance on the purpose of life. The Quran states: "And I did not create the jinn and mankind except to worship Me." (Quran, Adh-Dhariyat 51:56)

This verse clearly articulates that the primary purpose of human existence is to worship Allah. Worship in Islam is not limited to ritualistic acts but encompasses every aspect of life, from daily activities to personal interactions, all performed to please Allah. The Prophet Muhammad (peace be upon him) also emphasized the importance of intention in all actions, stating: "Actions are but by intentions, and every person will get what he intended." (Sahih Bukhari)

This Hadith highlights that the intention behind every action determines its value in the eyes of Allah, thereby giving every moment of life the potential to fulfill our divine purpose.

**The Importance of Worship and Obedience to Allah**

Worship in Islam is a comprehensive concept that includes acts of devotion like prayer, fasting, and charity, as well as everyday actions done to please Allah. Obedience to Allah's commands and following the Sunnah of the Prophet Muhammad (peace and blessings be upon him) are essential components of worship. This obedience is not just about following rules; it is a means of aligning oneself with the divine will and achieving a harmonious existence in this world and the Hereafter.

**How Understanding Purpose Can Transform Daily Activities into Acts of Worship**

When a Muslim understands that the purpose of life is to worship Allah, it transforms the mundane into the meaningful. Everyday activities such as eating, working, and interacting with others can become acts of worship with the right intention. For example, earning a livelihood to provide for one's family is considered a form of worship if it is done honestly and fulfills one's responsibilities as prescribed by Islam. This perspective shifts the focus from merely achieving worldly success to seeking spiritual fulfillment and divine reward in all aspects of life.

## 2.2 Aligning Personal Goals with Divine Purpose

Islam encourages Muslims to live a balanced life, where personal aspirations and goals are aligned with the ultimate purpose of worshiping Allah. This alignment ensures that every goal pursued has a spiritual dimension, making it beneficial in this life and rewarding in the Hereafter.

## Setting Personal and Professional Goals with Islamic Values in Mind

Islam encourages setting goals that reflect both worldly ambitions and spiritual objectives. Personal goals, such as career advancement, financial stability, or education, should be pursued within Islamic ethics and values. Professional aspirations should not lead to compromising one's faith or engaging in unethical practices. For instance, a Muslim pursuing a business career should adhere to fairness and honesty, avoiding unethical practices like usury (Riba) or deceit.

## How to Balance Worldly Aspirations with Spiritual Duties

Balancing worldly aspirations with spiritual duties requires mindfulness and prioritization. Islam teaches that while seeking success in worldly matters is permissible, it should not come at the expense of one's spiritual obligations. This balance can be achieved by organizing one's time to ensure that personal ambitions and religious duties are fulfilled. For example, a Muslim professional should allocate time for prayer, Quranic recitation, and community service, ensuring their pursuit of worldly success does not detract from their spiritual growth.

## Examples of Muslims Who Achieved Great Things by Aligning Their Goals with Their Faith

History is replete with examples of Muslims who achieved greatness by aligning their goals with their faith. Scholars like Imam Al-Ghazali and Ibn Sina made significant contributions to philosophy, medicine, and science while remaining deeply committed to their faith. Contemporary examples include Muslims who have excelled in various professions—medicine, law, academia—while adhering to Islamic principles and ethics. Their success demonstrates that it is possible to achieve worldly success without compromising one's religious values.

## 2.3 Living a Purpose-Driven Life

Living a purpose-driven life in Islam involves intentionality, mindfulness, and striving for excellence in all that one does. This approach ensures that Muslims remain focused on their divine purpose and seek to fulfill it through their actions, words, and thoughts.

### How Islam Encourages Living with Intention and Mindfulness

Islam places a strong emphasis on intention (Niyyah) in every action. Living with intention means being mindful of why one is doing something and ensuring that the intention aligns with seeking Allah's pleasure. This mindfulness helps prevent heedlessness and ensures one's actions are meaningful and purposeful. For example, when engaging in daily tasks, a Muslim is encouraged to be conscious of their intentions, making even routine acts of worship.

### The Concept of Ihsan (Excellence) and How It Applies to Everyday Life

Ihsan, or excellence, is a concept that encourages Muslims to strive for the best in everything they do. The Prophet Muhammad (peace and blessings be upon him) said: "Verily, Allah has prescribed Ihsan (excellence) in all things..." (Sahih Muslim)

Ihsan applies to all aspects of life, from worship to work and relationships to personal conduct. It means doing everything to the best of one's ability, with sincerity and a desire to please Allah. By embodying Ihsan, Muslims transform their actions into acts of devotion and contribute positively to their community and the world.

## Developing Habits That Reinforce a Sense of Purpose and Commitment

Developing habits reinforcing a sense of purpose and commitment is essential for a purpose-driven life. This includes regular prayer, Quranic study, and engaging in good deeds. It also involves cultivating positive habits such as gratitude, patience, and generosity. These habits help maintain focus on one's divine purpose and ensure continuous personal and spiritual growth. For example, setting aside time daily for self-reflection and Quranic recitation can help Muslims stay connected to their faith and purpose.

Finding purpose and meaning in Islam is not a one-time discovery but a continuous journey of aligning oneself with divine guidance and striving to fulfill the purpose of worshiping Allah. This chapter has explored how Islam provides a clear and comprehensive framework for understanding life's purpose, aligning personal goals with divine objectives, and living purpose-driven lives. By embracing these principles, a Muslim can experience a profound transformation, leading to a life of fulfillment, balance, and spiritual growth.

The next chapter, "Developing a Strong Moral Compass," will explore how Islamic teachings provide a framework for developing strong ethical values and a moral compass that guides personal behavior and decision-making in all aspects of life.

# Chapter Three

# Developing a Strong Moral Compass

A strong moral compass is essential for leading a life of integrity, righteousness, and purpose. In Islam, morality and ethics are deeply rooted in divine guidance provided by the Quran and the teachings of the Prophet Muhammad (peace be upon him). This chapter explores how Islamic teachings cultivate a strong moral foundation, emphasizing values such as honesty, integrity, patience, and compassion. By adhering to these values, Muslims can navigate life's challenges with clarity and confidence, fostering a life that aligns with the divine will.

## 3.1 Foundations of Islamic Ethics and Morality

Islamic ethics and morality are grounded in the belief that Allah is the ultimate source of all moral authority. The Quran and Sunnah serve as the primary sources of guidance, providing a comprehensive framework for ethical behavior in every aspect of life.

### Understanding Halal (Permissible) and Haram (Forbidden) in Daily Life

In Islam, actions and behaviors are classified into categories such as Halal (permissible) and Haram (forbidden). Halal encompasses all that is lawful and good, while Haram includes anything harmful or explicitly prohibited by Allah. Understanding these categories is crucial for developing a strong moral compass, as they provide clear guidelines on what is acceptable and unacceptable in a Muslim's daily life. For example, honesty, kindness, and justice are always encouraged, while lying, stealing, and injustice are strictly forbidden.

### The Role of the Quran and Sunnah in Guiding Ethical Behavior

The Quran and the Sunnah of the Prophet Muhammad (peace and blessings be upon him) serve as the ultimate sources of ethical guidance in Islam. The Quran provides explicit instructions on moral conduct, such as the importance of truthfulness, justice, and compassion. The Sunnah, which includes the sayings, actions, and approvals of the Prophet (peace and blessings be upon him), offers practical examples of how to implement these ethical principles in daily life. Together, they form a comprehensive moral framework that helps Muslims develop a strong ethical foundation.

### How Islamic Ethics Transform Personal Decision-Making Processes

Islamic ethics fundamentally transform how a Muslim approaches decision-making. When faced with a moral dilemma, a Muslim considers not only the legal permissibility (Halal or Haram) but also the ethical implications of their actions. This process involves consulting the Quran and Sunnah, seeking guidance through prayer (Istikhara), and considering the impact of their decisions on themselves and others. This ethical framework ensures that personal choices align with Islamic values, promoting a life of righteousness and integrity.

## 3.2 Cultivating Honesty, Integrity, and Trustworthiness

Honesty, integrity, and trustworthiness are core values in Islam that form the foundation of a strong moral character. These qualities are emphasized repeatedly in the Quran and Hadith, highlighting their importance in personal and social conduct.

## The Importance of Honesty and Integrity in Islam

Honesty and integrity are considered fundamental virtues in Islam. The Quran states: "O you who have believed, fear Allah and speak words of appropriate justice." (Quran, Al-Ahzab 33:70)

This verse underscores the importance of honesty and truthfulness in all matters. The Prophet Muhammad (peace be upon him) also emphasized the value of honesty, stating: "Truthfulness leads to righteousness, and righteousness leads to Paradise." (Sahih Bukhari)

These teachings highlight that honesty is not just a social virtue but a spiritual imperative that leads to divine reward.

## The Prophet Muhammad's (peace be upon him) Example as "Al-Amin" (the Trustworthy)

The Prophet Muhammad (peace be upon him) was known as "Al-Amin," which means "the trustworthy." Even before his prophethood, he was renowned for his honesty and integrity, earning the trust and respect of the people of Mecca. His example serves as a powerful model for Muslims, demonstrating the importance of upholding honesty and trustworthiness in all aspects of life. By following the Prophet's example, Muslims can cultivate a reputation for integrity and reliability, both in their personal and professional lives.

## Practical Steps to Cultivate These Qualities in Personal and Professional Life

Cultivating honesty, integrity, and trustworthiness requires conscious effort and commitment. Practical steps include being truthful in all communications, honoring commitments and promises, and avoiding deceitful practices, even when they appear advantageous. In professional settings, this may involve maintaining transparency in business dealings, treating colleagues with fairness and respect, and upholding ethical standards in all transactions. By consistently practicing these qualities, Muslims can build a strong moral character that reflects their faith.

## 3.3 Practicing Patience, Gratitude, and Humility

Patience, gratitude, and humility are key virtues in Islam that contribute to a strong moral character. These qualities help Muslims navigate life's challenges with grace and maintain a positive outlook, regardless of circumstances.

### The Significance of Sabr (Patience) in Overcoming Life's Challenges

Sabr, or patience, is a highly regarded virtue in Islam. The Quran repeatedly emphasizes the importance of patience in facing adversity: "O you who have believed, seek help through patience and prayer. Indeed, Allah is with the patient." (Quran, Al-Baqarah 2:153)

Patience is not merely passive endurance; it is an active state of perseverance and resilience in the face of difficulties. Practicing patience helps Muslims maintain faith and composure, trusting that Allah's wisdom and timing are perfect, even in challenging situations.

### Developing a Mindset of Gratitude (Shukr) for Personal Growth

Gratitude, or Shukr, is another essential quality in Islam that fosters personal growth and contentment. The Quran encourages gratitude, stating: "And [remember] when your Lord proclaimed, 'If you are grateful, I will surely increase you [in favor]; but if you deny, indeed, My punishment is severe.'" (Quran, Ibrahim 14:7)

Practicing gratitude involves recognizing and appreciating Allah's blessings, both big and small. By focusing on the positives and expressing thankfulness, Muslims can cultivate a sense of contentment and prevent feelings of entitlement or dissatisfaction.

## Humility as a Cornerstone of Islamic Character and Its Transformative Effects

Humility is a foundational virtue in Islam that counteracts arrogance and fosters a spirit of servitude to Allah. The Quran warns against pride and arrogance: "And turn not your face away from people with pride, nor walk in insolence through the earth. Verily, Allah does not like any arrogant boaster." (Quran, Luqman 31:18)

Humility involves recognizing one's limitations, relying on Allah for guidance and support, and treating others with respect and kindness. This humility transforms interactions and relationships, promoting a culture of mutual respect and understanding.

Developing a strong moral compass in Islam involves understanding and adhering to the ethical teachings of the Quran and Sunnah. By cultivating qualities such as honesty, integrity, patience, gratitude, and humility, Muslims can navigate life's challenges with clarity and confidence, fostering a life that aligns with divine will. This chapter has explored how Islamic ethics provide a comprehensive framework for personal and social conduct, guiding Muslims towards a life of righteousness, integrity, and spiritual fulfillment.

In the next chapter, we will focus on how one lays the foundation for inner peace, personal discipline, and ultimately, a deep and fulfilling relationship with the Creator.

# Chapter Four

# Avoiding Sins

The journey of personal transformation in Islam begins with the conscious effort to avoid sins. Sins create a barrier between the believer and Allah, diminishing the spiritual connection that is central to one's faith. To truly grow, it is essential to understand that staying away from sins is not just about avoiding punishment but about purifying the heart and aligning oneself with the values that bring one closer to Allah. By avoiding sinful behaviors and nurturing taqwa (God-consciousness), one lays the foundation for inner peace, personal discipline, and ultimately, a deep and fulfilling relationship with the Creator.

## 4.1 The Advice of 'Umar ibn Al-Khattab to Sa'd ibn Abi Waqqas

Sa'd ibn Waqqas (may Allah be pleased with him) was a beloved companion of the Prophet (peace and blessings be upon him), the commander-in-chief of the Muslim army dispatched to confront the Persians at Qadisiyyah. The Amirul Mu'minin, 'Umar ibn Al Khattab (may Allah be pleased with him), stood before the great army spread around him and bade them farewell. 'Umar said to Sa'd,

"O Sa'd! Do not allow any statement that you are the maternal uncle of the Messenger of Allah (peace and blessings be upon) or that you are the Companion of the Messenger of Allah (peace and blessings be upon) to distract you from Allah, the Almighty. Allah Almighty does not obliterate evil with evil but wipes out evil with good. O Sa'd! There is no connection between Allah and any of His Servants except obedience to Him. In the sight of Allah, all people, whether common or noble, are the same. Allah is their Lord, and they are His slaves, seeking elevation through taqwa (piety) and seeking to obtain what is good through obedience. Look at the way of the Messenger of Allah (peace and blessings be upon), from when he was sent until he left us, and adhere to it, for it is the proper way. That is my advice: if you ignore it and turn away from it, you will be one of the losers. I am ordering you and the troops with you to fear Allah in all circumstances, as fear of Allah is the best weapon against the enemy and the strongest weapon in war. I am commanding you and those with you to be more careful avoiding sin than avoiding your enemy. The Muslims are supported by their enemy's disobedience towards Allah. If it were not for that, we would not have any strength, as our numbers are not like theirs. If we were equally matched in sin, they would have an advantage over us in strength, and if we did not have an advantage over them by our virtue, we would not be able to defeat them by our strength."

## 4.2 Lessons From the Advice

The advice of 'Umar to Sa'd is a profound lesson in the transformative power of abstaining from sins. 'Umar, one of the greatest leaders in Islamic history, reminded Sa'd not to be distracted by the honor of being the Messenger of Allah's relative or companion but instead to focus on his relationship with Allah. His words highlight that the true measure of a person is not in status or lineage but in obedience and sincerity before Allah.

To transform oneself, one must adhere to the principle that good actions erase evil, while evil cannot erase other evils. Staying away from sins is not just about avoiding wrongdoing but replacing them with positive, righteous actions that please Allah. This is how one can purify oneself and maintain a state of spiritual elevation. 'Umar emphasized that in Allah's sight, all people are equal, and the only measure of distinction is piety (taqwa) and obedience to Him. By striving to follow the example of the Prophet Muhammad (peace and blessings be upon) and adhering to the path he laid out, one finds the proper way to transform one's inner state.

'Umar's advice also conveys that avoiding sin is more crucial than merely avoiding an external enemy, as the Muslims' strength ultimately lies in their righteousness and connection with Allah. He pointed out that the believers' victories were not due to their superior numbers or worldly power but were because of the disobedience of their enemies and the virtue of the Muslims. Thus, he urged Sa'd to fear Allah and be vigilant against sin, as righteousness is a weapon more powerful than any physical means.

This perspective shows us that self-transformation in Islam is a continuous struggle against the ego and sins while cultivating good deeds and fearing Allah in every circumstance. Through adhering to the path of the Prophet (peace and blessings be upon him) and maintaining a conscious effort to obey Allah, one can elevate oneself, foster personal growth, and attain success in this life and the Hereafter. 'Umar's words serve as a timeless reminder that the key to transformation is sincerity, avoiding sin, and always seeking the path of virtue.

## 4.3 How to Avoid Sins

Avoiding sins requires a combination of self-discipline, spiritual awareness, and consistent effort. Here are some practical ways to help you stay away from sins:

### (1) Strengthen Your Relationship with Allah

**Prayer**

Consistently performing the five daily prayers helps maintain a close connection with Allah and serves as a constant reminder of His presence.

**Du'a (Supplication)**

Regularly ask Allah for protection from sin and guidance towards righteousness. A sincere dua is a powerful tool for seeking Allah's help.

### Dhikr (Remembrance of Allah)

Engage in regular remembrance of Allah. Dhikr helps keep the heart occupied with good and reduces the inclination towards sin.

## (2) Gain Knowledge

### Understand Halal and Haram

Learning about what is permissible and what is forbidden in Islam helps one avoid sins more consciously. Knowledge also clarifies misconceptions and provides practical ways to live by Islamic teachings.

### Learn the Consequences

Understanding the negative consequences of sin, both in this life and in the Hereafter, can serve as a deterrent. Reflecting on the rewards for avoiding sins also provides motivation.

## (3) Reflect on Accountability and Hereafter

### Remember Death and the Day of Judgment

Reflecting on death and the Day of Judgment can help put life in perspective, reminding you of the ultimate accountability and the importance of righteous behavior.

### Reflect on Allah's Attributes

Consider Allah's qualities, such as His mercy and justice. This reflection can inspire hope in His forgiveness and fear of His justice, motivating you to avoid sin.

## (4) Guard Against Temptations

### Avoid Harmful Environments

Avoid places, activities, and people that lead you to sinful behavior. Choosing pious friends and encouraging each other to do good deeds can make a significant difference.

### Lower Your Gaze

Guarding your eyes against looking at inappropriate things helps protect your heart from temptation. Lowering the gaze, as instructed by Allah in the Quran, helps control desires.

## (5) Replace Bad Habits with Good Ones

### Do Good Deeds

Good deeds erase bad ones. Replace sinful habits with positive actions, such as charity, helping others, or acts of kindness. Engaging in these actions fills the time and energy otherwise wasted on sin.

### Keep Busy with Productive Activities

Idleness often leads to sinful behavior. Engage yourself in beneficial activities, hobbies, or learning new skills to keep your mind and body occupied with positive pursuits.

## (6) Develop Taqwa (God-Consciousness)

### Be Mindful of Allah at All Times

Cultivate a sense of Allah's presence in every situation. This mindfulness, known as taqwa, is the key to avoiding sin. Remind yourself that Allah is All-Seeing and All-Knowing, and this awareness helps you control your actions.

### Think Before You Act

Before doing anything, ask yourself whether it will please Allah. This simple reflection can prevent many sins.

## (7) Repent and Seek Forgiveness Regularly

### Istighfar (Seeking Forgiveness)

Constantly ask Allah for forgiveness. No one is perfect, and everyone slips at times. Making it a habit to seek forgiveness helps cleanse the heart and encourages you to do better.

### Don't Lose Hope in Allah's Mercy

Even if you sin, remember that Allah's mercy is vast. Sincere repentance with a firm intention not to repeat the sin can bring you back on track.

## (8) Fast and Engage in Voluntary Worship

### Fasting

Fasting, especially outside of Ramadan, helps train you to control your desires and build self-discipline. Here is a list of Sunnah fasts that are encouraged in Islam, based on the teachings and practices of the Prophet Muhammad (peace and blessings be upon him):

**1. Fasting on Mondays and Thursdays** — The Prophet (peace and blessings be upon him) regularly fasted on these days and said:

"Deeds are presented (to Allah) on Mondays and Thursdays, and I like my deeds to be presented while I am fasting." (Tirmidhi, 747)

**2. Fasting on the White Days (Ayyam Al-Beedh)** — These are the 13th, 14th, and 15th of each lunar month.

"It is recommended to fast on the 13th, 14th, and 15th days of each lunar month. (Abu Dawood, 2449)

**3. Fasting on the Day of Arafah (9th of Dhul-Hijjah)** — For those not performing Hajj, fasting on this day is highly recommended. "Fasting on the Day of Arafah expiates the sins of the previous year and the coming year." (Muslim, 1162)

**4. Fasting on Ashura (10th of Muharram) and the Day Before or After** — The Prophet (peace and blessings be upon him) encouraged fasting on the 10th of Muharram (Ashura) and also fasting on the 9th or 11th along with it.

"For fasting the day of Ashura, I hope that Allah will accept it as expiation for the year that went before." (Muslim)

**5. Fasting Six Days of Shawwal** — After completing Ramadan, fasting six additional days during Shawwal brings great reward.

"Whoever fasts Ramadan and then follows it with six days of Shawwal, it is as if he fasted for a lifetime." (Muslim, 1164)

**6. Fasting on the First Nine Days of Dhul-Hijjah** — The first nine days of Dhul-Hijjah, especially the Day of Arafah, are encouraged for fasting.

"There are no days in which righteous deeds are more beloved to Allah than these ten days (Dhul-Hijjah)." (Bukhari, 969)

**7. Fasting on the Middle of Sha'ban (15th of Sha'ban)** — Fasting on the 15th of Sha'ban (known as Nisf Sha'ban) is considered a Sunnah in some traditions, although its specific significance is debated. Many scholars still recommend fasting for those who regularly observe voluntary fasts.

**8. Fasting on Days of Repentance or Gratitude** — The Prophet (peace and blessings be upon him) would fast to express gratitude or as a form of repentance when seeking forgiveness from Allah.

These Sunnah fasts are not obligatory but highly recommended for spiritual growth and seeking Allah's reward.

**Voluntary Prayer**

Engage in optional prayers (Sunnah and Nafl). They act as a shield against sin and bring you closer to Allah. They are encouraged in Islam, based on the teachings and practices of the Prophet Muhammad (peace and blessings be upon him). Start with 2 Raka'hs and gradually increase them.

**1. Sunnah Mu'akkadah (Emphasized Sunnah Prayers):**

These are highly encouraged and strongly recommended prayers, though not obligatory. The Prophet (peace and blessings be upon him) performed them regularly.

**(1) Sunnah of Fajr** — 2 Rak'ahs before the obligatory Fajr prayer.

The Prophet (peace and blessings be upon him) said: "The two Rak'ahs before Fajr are better than the world and all that it contains." (Muslim, 725)

**(2) Sunnah of Dhuhr** — 4 Rak'ahs before the obligatory Dhuhr prayer (offered in 2 + 2 units), and 2 Rak'ahs after.

The Prophet (peace and blessings be upon him) said: — "Whoever prays four Rak'ahs before Dhuhr and four after it, the Fire will not touch him." (Tirmidhi, 428)

**(3) Sunnah of Maghrib** — 2 Rak'ahs after the obligatory Maghrib prayer.

**(4) Sunnah of Isha** — 2 Rak'ahs after the obligatory Isha prayer.

## 2. Sunnah Ghair Mu'akkadah (Non-Emphasized Sunnah Prayers):

These prayers are optional and not as strongly emphasized, but are still highly encouraged for additional reward.

**(1) Additional Rak'ahs before and after Dhuhr** — It is recommended to pray 2 Rak'ahs before and 2 Rak'ahs after Dhuhr in addition to the Sunnah Mu'akkadah.

**(2) Additional Rak'ahs after Maghrib** — Some scholars recommend an additional 2 Rak'ahs after the 2 Rak'ahs of Sunnah.

**(3) Additional Rak'ahs after Isha'** — It is recommended that 2 more Rak'ahs be offered in addition to the Sunnah Mu'akkadah.

## 3. Nafl (Voluntary) Prayers:

These are some optional prayers for additional rewards and spiritual closeness to Allah.

**(1) Tahajjud (Night Prayer)** — Prayed during the last third of the night before Fajr. There is no set number of Rak'ahs, but the Prophet (peace and blessings be upon him) often prayed in units of 2.

Allah says in the Qur'an: "And during a part of the night, pray Tahajjud beyond what is incumbent on you; perhaps your Lord will raise you to a position of great glory." (Qur'an, Al-Isra' 17:79)

Allah says: "And when My servants ask you, [O Muhammad], concerning Me - indeed I am near. I respond to the
invocation of the supplicant when he calls upon Me. So let them respond to Me [by obedience] and believe in Me that they may be [rightly] guided. (Qur'an, Al-Baqarah 2:186)

Make du'a and ask Allah for His forgiveness during this time.

**(2) Duha (Forenoon Prayer)** — Prayed after sunrise (15-20 minutes after sunrise) until before Dhuhr. It is usually prayed in 2 Rak'ahs, but more can be offered.

The Prophet (peace and blessings be upon him) said: "In the morning, charity is due on every joint bone of the body of every one of you. Every utterance of

Allah's glorification is an act of charity... and two Rak'ahs which one may pray in the Duha will suffice." (Muslim, 720)

**(3) Witr** — Offered after Isha and before Fajr, usually prayed as an odd number of Rak'ahs (1, 3, 5, or more).

The Prophet (peace and blessings be upon him) said: "Make Witr the last of your prayers at night." (Bukhari, 998)

**(4) Salat Al-Istikhara (Prayer for Guidance)** — Prayed when seeking guidance from Allah for any decision. It consists of two Rak'ahs, followed by a specific supplication (Dua of Istikhara).

The Prophet (peace and blessings be upon him) used to teach his companions this prayer for guidance in all matters.

**(5) Salat Al-Tawbah (Prayer for Repentance)** — A prayer offered to seek forgiveness from Allah for sins. It consists of two Rak'ahs, followed by sincere repentance and asking for forgiveness.

**(6) Salat Al-Hajat (Prayer for Need)** — This prayer is for when a person has a specific need and seeks help from Allah. It consists of two Rak'ahs, followed by a supplication for the need.

**(7) Salat Al-Tarawih (Ramadan Night Prayers)** — Prayed on the nights of Ramadan, usually in sets of 2 Rak'ahs. It is commonly prayed in congregation in sets of 8 or 20 Rak'ahs.

**(8) Salat Al-Eid (Eid Prayers)** — Prayed on the morning of Eid Al-Fitr and Eid Al-Adha, consisting of 2 Rak'ahs performed in congregation.

**(9) Salat Al-Tahiyyat Al-Masjid (Greeting the Mosque Prayer)** — Prayed when entering a mosque, consisting of 2 Rak'ahs before sitting down.

**(10) Salat after Wudu'** — Prayed 2 Rak'ahs after performing wudu'.

Narrated Abu Hurayrah: At the time of the Fajr prayer, the Prophet (peace and blessings be upon him asked Bilal, "Tell me of the best deed you did after embracing Islam, for I heard your footsteps in front of me in Paradise." Bilal replied, "I did not do anything worth mentioning except that whenever I performed ablution during the day or night, I prayed after that ablution as much as was written for me." (Bukhari, 1149)

While not obligatory, these Sunnah and Nafl prayers carry immense rewards and bring a person closer to Allah. They help strengthen one's connection with Allah and bring peace and tranquility through consistent, voluntary worship.

## 9. Daily Quran Recitation

Daily Quran recitation profoundly impacts personal transformation, both spiritually and emotionally. Start with half a page to a page daily and gradually increase the reading until you can consistently read 20 pages (one juz) to 40 pages (2 juz) daily.

Narrated Abdullah ibn Amr ibn al-'As: Yazid ibn Abdullah said that Abdullah ibn Amr asked the Prophet (peace and blessings be upon him: In how many days should I complete the recitation of the whole Qur'an, Messenger of Allah? He replied: In one month. He said: I am more energetic about completing it in a period less than this. He repeated these words and lessened the period until he said: Complete its recitation in seven days. He again said: I am more energetic about completing it in a period less than this. The Prophet (peace and blessings be upon him) said: He who finishes the recitation of the Qur'an in less than three days does not understand it.

Regularly reading and reflecting on the Quran brings numerous benefits, leading to a deeper connection with Allah and shaping one's character and life. Here are some key ways daily Quran recitation can transform a person.

### (1) Spiritual Nourishment

The Quran is the direct word of Allah, and regular recitation provides a source of spiritual nourishment. It strengthens a person's faith (Iman) and fosters a deep connection with the Creator. Consistent engagement with the Quran makes believers feel closer to Allah, bringing peace, contentment, and purpose.

### (2) Guidance for Life

The Quran guides all aspects of life, offering wisdom on how to live ethically, treat others with kindness, and navigate personal and societal challenges. Daily recitation allows one to continuously absorb and implement these teachings, leading to conscious decision-making and a life by Islamic principles.

### (3) Emotional Healing and Peace

The Quran is described as a cure for what is in the hearts (Qur'an, At-Tawba 10:57). Daily recitation has a calming effect, helping to relieve stress, anxiety, and sadness. The rhythmic recitation and reflection on its verses bring tranquility to the soul, providing emotional balance and resilience in life's hardships.

### (4) Personal Reflection and Self-Improvement

Regular recitation encourages self-reflection (Tadabbur), inspiring personal growth and self-improvement. By reflecting on the verses, believers can assess their behavior, identify areas that need improvement, and strive to adopt the qualities of patience, gratitude, humility, and sincerity. It becomes a constant reminder to strive for excellence in character.

### (5) Strengthens Morality and Ethics

The Quran emphasizes justice, kindness, honesty, and other moral virtues. As people engage with these themes daily, they are reminded of their moral obligations and the importance of integrity. This consistent reinforcement helps cultivate a strong ethical framework, making people more mindful of their actions.

### (6) Increases Mindfulness and Consciousness (Taqwa)

Daily Quran recitation keeps a person mindful of Allah's presence and conscious of their accountability in the Hereafter. This heightened awareness, known as Taqwa, shields against sin and wrong behavior, motivating believers to act with righteousness in their daily interactions and decisions.

## (7) Consistency in Worship and Discipline

Regular recitation builds a habit of consistency, which is greatly valued in Islam. The daily discipline of reciting the Quran encourages time management, self-control, and the importance of balancing worldly tasks with spiritual duties. This consistency in worship also strengthens a person's relationship with Allah and brings barakah (blessings) into their life.

## (8) Language of the Heart

For non-Arabic speakers, regular recitation also fosters a connection with the language of revelation. Even if the meanings are not fully understood, reciting the Quran in its original Arabic form uniquely impacts the heart and soul. The transformation is even deeper for those who try to understand its meaning, as the Quran's teachings are directly absorbed into their worldview.

## (9) Enhances Patience and Perseverance

The Quran frequently discusses patience (Sabr) and perseverance (Istiqamah). Engaging with these messages daily can transform a person's ability to cope with difficulties and challenges, reminding them of the rewards of steadfastness and trust in Allah's plan.

## 10. Preparation for the Hereafter

Daily Quran recitation helps a person keep their focus on the Hereafter (Akhirah) rather than becoming overly absorbed in the material world. This regular reminder about the transitory nature of worldly life encourages a balanced approach to life, prompting one to prioritize deeds that will benefit them in the Hereafter.

Daily Quran recitation is a powerful tool for personal transformation, impacting the heart and the mind. It cultivates spiritual growth, moral integrity, and emotional well-being while fostering a deeper connection with Allah.

Through the continuous practice of reciting and reflecting on the Quran, individuals can shape their lives by divine guidance, transforming themselves into better, more conscious Muslims who strive for success in this world and the Hereafter.

## 11. Reflect on the Example of the Prophet and Companions

### Follow the Sunnah

Look at how the Prophet Muhammad (peace and blessings be upon him) lived and avoided sin. His character serves as the best example for Muslims.

### Study the Lives of the Companions

Reflect on the Companions' actions, such as 'Umar ibn al-Khattab's advice to Sa'd ibn Abi Waqqas about avoiding sin. They lived with the Prophet (peace and blessings be upon him) and applied his teachings practically in their lives.

By consistently applying these principles, one can reduce one's inclination toward sin and develop a lifestyle centered around Allah's worship and obedience. The path to avoiding sin requires vigilance, humility, and persistence, but it leads to peace of mind, closeness to Allah, and success in this life and the Hereafter.

# Chapter Five

# Consistency in Islam

Consistency, or *Istiqamah* in Arabic, is a fundamental concept in Islam that denotes steadfastness, perseverance, and adherence to a straight path of faith and righteous conduct. It is a principle that permeates various aspects of Islamic teachings, encouraging Muslims to maintain a steady and unwavering commitment to their faith, ethics, and duties, regardless of circumstances. The concept of consistency is deeply embedded in both the Qur'an and the Sunnah (traditions of the Prophet Muhammad, peace and blessings be upon him), reflecting its importance in the life of a Muslim.

## 5.1 Consistency in Worship and Acts of Devotion

One of the primary areas where consistency is emphasized in Islam is in worship and acts of devotion. The daily rituals prescribed in Islam—such as the five daily prayers (Salah), fasting during the month of Ramadan, giving charity (Zakat), and the annual pilgrimage to Mecca (Hajj)—require regular and consistent practice. These acts are not meant to be performed sporadically or when convenient but rather with regularity and devotion, demonstrating a continual commitment to Allah.

The Qur'an highlights the importance of regular worship: "Establish prayer at the two ends of the day and at the approach of the night. Indeed, good deeds do away with misdeeds. That is a reminder for those who remember." (Qur'an, Hud 11:114)

This ayah emphasizes the importance of maintaining regular prayers as a means of spiritual purification and maintaining a strong connection with Allah.

The Prophet Muhammad (peace be upon him) also emphasized the importance of consistency in worship. In a well-known hadith, he said: "The most beloved deeds to Allah are those that are consistent, even if they are small." [Sahih Bukhari]

This hadith highlights that Allah values consistency in worship and good deeds more than sporadic, large acts. The emphasis is on steady, continuous actions that reflect a sincere commitment to one's faith and devotion to Allah.

## 5.2 Consistency in Good Character and Moral Conduct

Consistency in Islam is not limited to acts of worship but extends to maintaining good character and ethical behavior in all aspects of life. Islam teaches that a Muslim should strive to embody virtues such as honesty, patience, kindness, and humility consistently, regardless of external circumstances. This consistency in character is a reflection of a person's inner faith and commitment to living according to Islamic principles.

The Prophet Muhammad (peace be upon him) is reported to have said: "The best among you are those who have the best manners and character." (Sahih Bukhari)

Maintaining good character consistently, especially in the face of challenges or adversity, is a hallmark of a true believer. For example, being honest and fair in business dealings, showing kindness to others, and maintaining patience in difficult situations are all actions that should be performed consistently to reflect the integrity and moral uprightness that Islam advocates.

## 5.3 Consistency in Seeking Knowledge and Personal Growth

Islam encourages continuous personal growth and the pursuit of knowledge, which requires a consistent effort. The Prophet Muhammad (peace be upon him) emphasized the importance of seeking knowledge throughout one's life: "Seeking knowledge is an obligation upon every Muslim." (Ibn Majah)

This hadith underscores the value Islam places on knowledge and education, viewing it as a lifelong endeavor that requires perseverance and dedication. Consistency in seeking knowledge means continually striving to learn, reflect, and improve oneself, both spiritually and intellectually. It involves regularly reading the Qur'an, studying the Hadith, attending religious lectures, and engaging in self-reflection to understand and practice Islamic teachings better.

## 5.4 Consistency in Social Responsibilities and Community Engagement

Islam teaches that a Muslim's life is not only about personal devotion but also about contributing positively to society. Consistency in fulfilling social responsibilities and engaging in community service is highly encouraged in Islam. This includes helping those in need, participating in charitable activities, promoting justice, and working towards the betterment of society.

The Prophet Muhammad (peace and blessings be upon him) said: "The best of people are those that bring the most benefit to the rest of mankind." (Daraqutni)

This hadith illustrates that consistent engagement in acts that benefit others is highly valued in Islam. It calls on Muslims to be active participants in their communities, consistently advocating for and contributing to the welfare of others.

## 5.5 Consistency in Patience and Perseverance

Islam teaches that life is filled with tests and trials, and it is through patience and perseverance that one can overcome difficulties. Consistency in patience, especially in the face of adversity, is a key virtue in Islam. The Qur'an frequently reminds believers of the importance of remaining steadfast and patient: "O you who have believed, seek help through patience and prayer. Indeed, Allah is with the patient." (Qur'an, Al-Baqarah 2:153)

This ayah encourages Muslims to consistently practice patience and seek solace in prayer during challenging times. It is through consistent patience that a believer strengthens their faith and trust in Allah's wisdom and mercy.

## 5.6 The Role of Consistency in Building Faith (Iman)

In Islam, Faith (Iman) is not static but rather dynamic, requiring constant nurturing and reinforcement through consistent worship, good deeds, and ethical conduct. The more consistently a person engages in acts of worship and avoids sinful behavior, the stronger their faith becomes. Conversely, neglecting regular worship or engaging in sinful behavior can weaken one's faith.

The Prophet Muhammad (peace be upon him) emphasized the importance of maintaining a steady commitment to faith: "Faith wears out in the heart of anyone just as clothes wear out, so ask Allah to renew the faith in your hearts." (Mustadrak al-Hakim)

This hadith highlights the need for consistency in renewing one's faith through regular acts of worship, prayer, and self-reflection.

## 5.7 Practical Ways to Cultivate Consistency in Islam

To cultivate consistency in one's Islamic practice, here are some practical steps that Muslims can take:

**Set Realistic Goals**

Start with achievable goals for acts of worship and good deeds, and gradually increase them over time. For example, begin with a few verses of Qur'an reading daily and slowly increase the amount.

**Develop a Routine**

Establish a daily routine that includes regular prayers, Qur'an recitation, and other forms of worship to ensure these acts become habitual.

## Seek Support

Engage with a supportive community or group that encourages consistent practice of faith, such as attending regular study circles or prayer groups.

## Reflect Regularly

Regular self-reflection and assessment help identify areas for improvement and reinforce the commitment to consistency in faith and practice.

## Pray for Guidance

Consistently seek Allah's guidance and support through supplication (du'a), asking for strength and perseverance in maintaining a steady practice of faith.

Consistency is a cornerstone of Islamic teachings that permeates all aspects of a Muslim's life, from worship and personal development to social responsibility and ethical conduct. The concept of *Istiqamah* encourages Muslims to remain steadfast, committed, and unwavering in their faith and actions. Through consistency, a Muslim not only strengthens their relationship with Allah but also contributes to the betterment of themselves and society. This unwavering commitment to consistency reflects a deep understanding of Islam's holistic approach to life, where every action, no matter how small, is an opportunity to draw closer to Allah and embody the principles of the faith.

# Chapter Six
# Forming Good Habits

Islam provides comprehensive guidance on every aspect of life, including developing good habits and eliminating harmful ones. Habit formation in Islam is closely tied to self-discipline and the pursuit of righteousness. By integrating teachings from the Qur'an and the Sunnah (the teachings and practices of the Prophet Muhammad, peace be upon him), Islam offers a framework for cultivating positive habits that lead to personal growth, spiritual well-being, and social harmony. This chapter explores the principles of forming good habits in Islam, emphasizing the importance of intention, consistency, and community support.

## 6.1 The Importance of Intentions in Habit Formation

In Islam, every action is judged by its intention. The formation of good habits begins with a sincere intention (niyyah). Islam teaches that intentions should align with seeking the pleasure of Allah, which gives a spiritual dimension to habit formation. This concept is highlighted in a well-known hadith: "Actions are judged by intentions, so each person will receive what they intended." (Sahih Bukhari and Sahih Muslim)

This hadith emphasizes the importance of having a clear and sincere intention behind every action. The concept of intention is crucial in forming good habits because it aligns actions with a higher purpose—seeking the pleasure of Allah. When Muslims intend to form a good habit, such as regular prayer, charitable giving, or reciting the Qur'an, they do so not merely for personal gain but to fulfill their spiritual duties and grow closer to Allah. This spiritual focus gives habit formation a deeper meaning and purpose, enhancing motivation and commitment.

When forming a habit, Muslims should ask themselves, "Is this action bringing me closer to being the person Allah wants me to be?" This reflection helps reinforce the habit with a clear, spiritually driven purpose.

By setting a clear intention to form a good habit—whether it is regular prayer, charitable giving, or seeking knowledge—Muslims align their actions with their spiritual goals. This alignment reinforces the habit, making it more meaningful and sustainable.

## 6.2 Consistency and Persistence in Developing Good Habits

Islam teaches the importance of consistency and persistence in developing good habits. *Istiqamah* (steadfastness) is central to Islamic teachings, encouraging Muslims to remain firm in their faith and practice, regardless of challenges or distractions.

The Prophet Muhammad (peace be upon him) highlighted the value of consistency in deeds: "The most beloved deeds to Allah are those that are done consistently, even if they are few." (Sahih Bukhari)

This hadith underscores that Allah values small, consistent actions more than sporadic, large actions. In the context of habit formation, this principle encourages Muslims to start with manageable and sustainable practices and gradually build upon them. For example, instead of trying to memorize large portions of the Qur'an in a short period, one might start with a few verses each day and consistently review them. Making the habit simple and manageable becomes easier to maintain, eventually becoming a natural part of one's daily routine.

Consistency in performing acts of worship, such as the five daily prayers, fasting during Ramadan, or giving regular charity, helps solidify these practices into lasting habits. Over time, these actions become integral to a Muslim's daily routine, strengthening their spiritual connection and discipline.

## 6.3 Encouragement to Start Small and Build Gradually

Islam acknowledges the human condition and encourages gradual progress in developing good habits. The Prophet Muhammad (peace be upon him) provided practical advice on starting small and building gradually to avoid burnout or discouragement. He understood the importance of manageable steps in forming long-lasting habits.

A hadith reflects this approach: "Take up good deeds only as much as you are able, for the best deeds are those done regularly even if they are few." (Sunan Ibn Majah)

This hadith advises Muslims to begin with actions they can consistently perform. When forming new habits, it is important to start small and gradually increase the effort as the habit becomes more ingrained. This method prevents overwhelm and helps maintain the habit over the long term.

For example, a person trying to develop the habit of waking up early for the Fajr prayer may start by setting their alarm 15 minutes earlier than usual and gradually adjust as they become accustomed to the new routine.

## 6.4 The Role of Environment and Community in Habit Formation

Islam stresses the importance of surrounding oneself with positive influences and creating an environment that promotes spiritual well-being. The Prophet Muhammad (peace be upon him) said: "A person is upon the religion of their close friend, so let one of you look at whom they befriend." (Sunan Abu Dawood)

This hadith highlights the importance of choosing one's environment and companions wisely, as they significantly impact one's behavior and habits. To form good habits, Muslims should create an environment that supports their goals. This could include:

## Physical Environment

Keeping a clean and dedicated prayer space, placing a Qur'an in a visible and accessible location, or having Islamic books on hand encourages regular engagement in spiritual practices.

## Social Environment

Surrounding oneself with pious and supportive friends who encourage good deeds and discourage bad habits. Joining study circles, attending mosque prayers, engaging in community activities, engaging in charity, or seeking knowledge encourages similar behaviors and can provide the necessary support and motivation to maintain good habits.

Islam also emphasizes the importance of creating a positive environment at home and within the family. Encouraging good habits in children from a young age, such as praying together, reciting the Qur'an, and engaging in acts of kindness, helps instill these as lifelong habits.

# 6.5 Self-Discipline and Control Over Desires

Islam places significant emphasis on self-discipline and controlling one's desires. A key component of habit formation is the ability to resist temptations and remain steadfast in the face of challenges. Fasting during Ramadan is a prime example of how Islam teaches self-control and discipline. Fasting involves refraining from food and drink and requires abstaining from negative behaviors, such as lying, backbiting, and arguing.

The Qur'an emphasizes the importance of self-control: "And those who restrain anger and pardon the people—Allah loves the doers of good." (Qur'an, AleImran 3:134)

Through self-discipline, Muslims learn to control their impulses and avoid behaviors that are harmful to themselves or others. This control extends to forming habits that require effort and persistence, such as maintaining regular prayers, giving charity, or avoiding sinful behavior.

## 6.6 Making Habits Attractive and Satisfying

In Islam, good habits are inherently attractive because they are associated with spiritual rewards and the pleasure of Allah. However, Muslims can also use immediate rewards to reinforce these habits. For instance, after completing a session of Qur'an recitation or performing extra prayers, one could reward themselves with a small treat or enjoyable activity. This immediate reward creates a positive association with the habit, making it more attractive and motivating to continue.

Moreover, reflecting on the spiritual benefits and rewards of certain habits can increase their attractiveness. The Qur'an and Hadith often mention the immense rewards for acts like fasting, charity, and prayer. For example, the reward for fasting is particularly emphasized: "Fasting is a shield. The one observing fasting should avoid intimate relations with his wife and should not behave foolishly and impudently, and if somebody fights with him or abuses him, he should tell him twice, 'I am fasting.'" (Sahih Bukhari)*

Understanding these spiritual rewards can make good habits more appealing, providing a strong incentive to maintain them consistently.

## 6.7 Reducing Friction to Make Good Habits Easier

Islam similarly encourages believers to facilitate good deeds and avoid making things difficult. The Prophet Muhammad (peace be upon him) advised: "Make things easy, do not make things difficult." (Sahih Bukhari)

Muslims can simplify the steps required to perform good habits to reduce friction and make them easier. For instance, preparing one's prayer clothes or setting up a prayer area the night before can make it easier to wake up for Fajr prayer. Keeping a charity box at home can simplify the process of giving regularly. The idea is to minimize obstacles and make the desired habit as convenient as possible.

## 6.8 Leveraging Accountability and Community Support

In Islam, the concept of mutual accountability and community support is emphasized. Muslims are encouraged to help each other in righteousness and piety: "Help one another in acts of righteousness and piety, and do not help one another in sin and transgression." (Qur'an, Al-Mai'da 5:2)

A supportive community or a "habit partner" can provide motivation, encouragement, and accountability. Muslims can join prayer groups, participate in study circles, or form support groups to memorize the Quran. These communal activities foster a sense of accountability and provide a support network to encourage consistency in good habits.

## 6.9 Seeking Forgiveness and Renewing Intentions

Islam recognizes that humans are fallible and prone to making mistakes. The concept of *Tawbah* (repentance) encourages Muslims to seek forgiveness for their shortcomings and renew their intentions. This process is crucial in habit formation, allowing for self-reflection and course correction.

The Prophet Muhammad (peace be upon him) said: "Every son of Adam sins, and the best of those who sin are those who repent." (Sunan Ibn Majah)

When Muslims slip or fall short in maintaining good habits, Islam encourages them not to despair but to seek forgiveness and renew their efforts. This teaching fosters resilience and perseverance, essential qualities in forming and maintaining good habits.

## 6.10 Reward and Motivation in Habit Formation

Islam offers both spiritual and worldly rewards for good deeds and habits, which motivate Muslims to persist in their efforts. *Ajr* (reward) is a powerful motivator in Islamic teachings, encouraging believers to engage in consistent good practices with the promise of divine reward.

The Quran states: "Indeed, those who have believed and done righteous deeds—Allah will grant them a reward that never ends." (Qur'an, Fussilat 41:8)

This ayah highlights the eternal reward awaiting those who consistently perform good deeds. The promise of Allah's reward motivates Muslims to maintain their good habits, knowing that Allah recognizes and values their efforts. This spiritual incentive encourages believers to stay committed to their positive actions, fostering a mindset that looks beyond immediate gratification and focuses on long-term spiritual growth and fulfillment.

## 6.11 Utilizing Daily Rituals for Habit Building

Islam's daily rituals, such as the five daily prayers (Salah), offer a practical framework for habit formation. These prayers, performed at specific times throughout the day, remind Muslims to pause, reflect, and reconnect with their Creator. The structure of the daily prayers fosters a sense of discipline and routine, which can be extended to other aspects of a Muslim's life.

For instance, incorporating short supplications (du'as) or recitations of the Qur'an after each prayer can help build a habit of regular spiritual reflection and mindfulness. The rhythm of daily prayers also encourages time management and the development of a balanced lifestyle, integrating both spiritual and worldly responsibilities.

By utilizing these daily rituals, Muslims can anchor other good habits around their prayer times, creating a structured routine that promotes holistic development.

## 6.12 Habit of Gratitude and Positive Thinking

Islam teaches the importance of gratitude (shukr) and positive thinking as habits that can transform a person's outlook on life. The Qur'an encourages believers to be grateful for the countless blessings bestowed upon them by Allah: "And [remember] when your Lord proclaimed: 'If you are grateful, I will surely increase you [in favor]; but if you deny, indeed, My punishment is severe.'" (Qur'an, Ibrahim 14:7)

This ayah highlights the importance of gratitude as a habit that pleases Allah and leads to increased blessings. By consistently practicing gratitude, Muslims develop a positive mindset that recognizes and appreciates the good in their lives, fostering a sense of contentment and reducing feelings of envy or dissatisfaction.

The habit of positive thinking is further reinforced by Islamic teachings that encourage believers to trust in Allah's wisdom and maintain hope, even in challenging circumstances. This mindset is encapsulated in the hadith: "Wondrous is the affair of the believer, for there is good for him in every matter, and this is not the case with anyone except the believer. If he is happy, he thanks Allah, and there is good for him; and if he is harmed, he shows patience, and there is good for him." (Sahih Muslim)

By cultivating gratitude and positive thinking habits, Muslims strengthen their resilience and ability to navigate life's challenges with grace and faith.

## 6.13 Accountability and Self-Monitoring

Islam encourages self-monitoring and accountability as part of habit formation. The concept of *Muhasabah* (self-accountability) involves regularly assessing one's actions and intentions to ensure they align with Islamic teachings and values. This process of self-reflection helps identify areas for improvement and reinforces positive behaviors.

The Qur'an reminds believers of the importance of self-accountability: "O you who have believed, fear Allah. And let every soul look to what it has put forth for tomorrow—and fear Allah. Indeed, Allah is Acquainted with what you do." (Qur'an, Al-Hashr 59:18)

By regularly reflecting on their actions, Muslims can hold themselves accountable for their habits and make necessary adjustments to align their behavior with their spiritual goals. This practice helps reinforce positive habits and discourages negative behaviors.

Islam provides a holistic approach to habit formation, emphasizing the importance of intentions, consistency, gradual progress, self-discipline, and accountability. By integrating these principles into their daily lives, Muslims are encouraged to develop habits that enhance their personal and spiritual growth and contribute positively to their families, communities, and society. The teachings of Islam offer a comprehensive framework for cultivating habits that lead to a balanced, purposeful, and fulfilling life, always keeping in mind the ultimate goal of pleasing Allah and attaining success in this world and the Hereafter.

The next chapter, "Building a Positive Mindset and Inner Peace," will focus on how Islamic teachings encourage a positive mindset, emotional resilience, and inner peace, essential for personal growth and well-being.

# Chapter Seven
# Building a Positive Mindset and Inner Peace

A positive mindset and inner peace are crucial for overall well-being and personal growth. Islam provides a holistic approach to cultivating a positive attitude and achieving tranquility of the heart. Through teachings that emphasize faith, trust in Allah (Tawakkul), gratitude, and remembrance of Allah (Dhikr), Islam offers tools and practices that help Muslims maintain emotional resilience and mental clarity, even in the face of life's challenges. This chapter explores how adopting Islamic principles can foster a positive mindset and cultivate a lasting sense of inner peace.

## 7.1 The Power of Positive Thinking in Islam

Islam encourages a positive outlook on life, grounded in faith and the belief that Allah's wisdom is beyond human understanding. This positive thinking stems from the conviction that every event, whether perceived as good or bad, is part of Allah's divine plan and holds a deeper purpose.

### Quranic Guidance on Maintaining Hope and Optimism

The Quran repeatedly encourages believers to remain hopeful and optimistic, even during difficult times. For example, Allah says: "So, verily, with the hardship, there is relief. Verily, with the hardship, there is relief." (Quran, Ash-Sharh 94:5-6)

These verses remind Muslims that hardships are temporary and that ease and relief will follow. This divine assurance encourages believers to maintain a hopeful outlook, trusting that Allah's wisdom encompasses all situations, and every difficulty comes with ease and growth.

## How Islamic Teachings Promote a Growth Mindset and Resilience

A growth mindset, which focuses on learning, self-improvement, and resilience, is integral to Islamic teachings. The Prophet Muhammad (peace be upon him) emphasized resilience and perseverance in the face of adversity, stating: "Wondrous is the affair of the believer, for it is good for him in every matter, and this is not the case with anyone except the believer. If he is happy, he thanks Allah, and there is good for him. If he is harmed, he shows patience, and there is good for him." (Sahih Muslim)

This Hadith illustrates the transformative power of maintaining a growth mindset, where every experience, whether positive or negative, becomes an opportunity for spiritual and personal growth.

## Stories of Companions and Scholars Who Exemplified Positive Thinking

Throughout Islamic history, numerous examples of companions and scholars embodied positive thinking and resilience. For instance, the Prophet's companion, Abu Bakr As-Siddiq (may Allah be pleased with him), demonstrated unwavering faith and optimism during times of trial, such as the early days of Islam and the migration to Medina. Similarly, scholars like Imam Ahmad ibn Hanbal showed remarkable perseverance and positivity, even when faced with persecution. Their stories are powerful reminders of how maintaining a positive mindset can lead to personal and spiritual triumph.

## 7.2 Achieving Inner Peace Through Remembrance of Allah (Dhikr)

Dhikr, or the remembrance of Allah, is a profound spiritual practice in Islam that helps achieve inner peace and tranquility. By continuously remembering Allah, a Muslim nurtures a deep connection with the Creator, which brings comfort and solace to the heart.

### The Spiritual and Psychological Benefits of Dhikr

Dhikr has both spiritual and psychological benefits. Spiritually, it strengthens a Muslim's connection with Allah, reminding them of His presence, mercy, and power. Psychologically, Dhikr provides a sense of calm and reduces anxiety by focusing the mind on the divine. The Quran mentions: "Verily, in the remembrance of Allah do hearts find rest." (Quran, Ar-Ra'd 13:28)

This verse underscores the transformative power of Dhikr in calming the heart and achieving inner peace. Regular remembrance fosters a sense of security and trust in Allah's plan, reducing feelings of worry and uncertainty.

### Techniques for Incorporating Remembrance into Daily Routines

Incorporating Dhikr into daily routines can be done in various ways, such as through the repetition of phrases like "SubhanAllah" (Glory be to Allah), "Alhamdulillah" (Praise be to Allah), and "Allahu Akbar" (Allah is the Greatest). Muslims can also engage in morning and evening supplications (Adhkar), read and reflect on the Quran, and perform additional voluntary prayers (Nafl). By making Dhikr a regular part of daily life, Muslims can maintain a constant awareness of Allah's presence and cultivate peace and tranquility.

## The Impact of a Peaceful Mind on Overall Life Satisfaction and Transformation

A peaceful mind, nurtured through Dhikr and remembrance of Allah, positively impacts overall life satisfaction. When Muslims maintain a state of inner tranquility, they are better equipped to handle life's challenges with patience and wisdom. This inner peace transforms how one interacts with others, makes decisions, and perceives life's trials, leading to a more fulfilled and balanced life.

## 7.3 Overcoming Negative Emotions and Thoughts

Islam provides practical guidance on managing and overcoming negative emotions and thoughts, such as anger, envy, and despair. By applying these teachings, Muslims can cultivate emotional resilience and maintain a positive outlook.

## Islamic Teachings on Managing Anger, Envy, and Other Negative Emotions

Islam teaches specific methods for managing negative emotions. The Prophet Muhammad (peace be upon him) provided practical advice for controlling anger, such as: "If one of you becomes angry while standing, let him sit down. If the anger leaves him, (that is good); otherwise, let him lie down." (Sunan Abu Dawood)

Envy (Hasad) is also discouraged, as it leads to spiritual and social harm. The Prophet (peace be upon him) said: "Beware of envy, for it devours good deeds just as fire devours wood." (Sunan Abu Dawood)

By addressing these emotions directly and offering practical advice, Islam provides tools for maintaining emotional health and fostering a positive mindset.

## Practical Strategies for Cultivating Emotional Intelligence

Cultivating emotional intelligence involves self-awareness, self-regulation, empathy, and social skills—all qualities Islam encourages. Muslims are encouraged to engage in self-reflection (Muhasabah), seek forgiveness for their shortcomings, and work on developing patience and compassion. Regular prayer, recitation of the Quran, and seeking counsel from wise and knowledgeable individuals are also practical strategies for managing emotions and cultivating emotional intelligence.

## The Role of Self-Reflection (Muraqabah) in Personal Development

Muraqabah, or self-reflection, is an Islamic practice that involves introspection and accountability for one's actions. By regularly examining their thoughts, intentions, and behaviors, Muslims can identify areas for improvement and make conscious efforts to align themselves with Islamic teachings. This practice fosters personal development and emotional resilience, allowing individuals to overcome negative emotions and thoughts more effectively.

Building a positive mindset and achieving inner peace are essential components of personal growth and spiritual development in Islam. Muslims can cultivate emotional resilience and tranquility through the power of positive thinking, remembrance of Allah, and effective management of negative emotions. This chapter has explored how Islamic teachings provide a comprehensive approach to fostering a positive outlook and maintaining inner peace, contributing to overall life satisfaction and transformation.

The next chapter, "The Role of Worship in Personal Growth," will discuss how Islamic acts of worship, such as prayer, fasting, and charity, contribute to personal development and spiritual growth, fostering a deeper connection with Allah and enhancing one's overall well-being.

# Chapter Eight

# The Role of Worship in Personal Growth

Worship in Islam is not merely a set of rituals; it is a comprehensive way of life that fosters personal growth, spiritual development, and a deep connection with Allah. Acts of worship such as Salah (prayer), Sawm (fasting), Zakat (charity), and Hajj (pilgrimage) are designed to cultivate discipline, mindfulness, empathy, and a sense of community. This chapter explores how these acts of worship contribute to personal development, enhance spiritual awareness, and transform an individual's character and conduct.

## 8.1 Prioritizing Worship of Allah Most High

Abu Hurairah narrated that the Messenger of Allah (peace and blessings be upon him) said: "Indeed Allah, Most High said: 'O son of Adam! Devote yourself to My worship, I will fill your chest with riches and alleviate your poverty. And if you do not do so, then I will fill your hands with problems and not alleviate your poverty.'" [At-Tirmidhi]

This hadith conveys a profound message about prioritizing worship and devotion to Allah. In the hadith, Allah addresses humankind, saying:

## Devotion to Worship

The hadith emphasizes the need to devote oneself to worshipping Allah, not just in ritual acts but also in one's heart and actions. By prioritizing worship, a person aligns their life with a higher purpose, which brings inner fulfillment and spiritual richness.

## Promise of Fulfillment

Allah promises that if one devotes themselves to His worship, He will fill their chest with riches—interpreted as contentment, peace of mind, and blessings. This spiritual wealth alleviates not just material poverty but also the deeper sense of lack or dissatisfaction in life.

## Warning Against Neglecting Worship

If a person neglects worship and becomes engrossed in worldly pursuits, the hadith warns that Allah will fill their hands with problems. This suggests that focusing solely on worldly matters without spiritual grounding leads to stress, anxiety, and endless struggles without a sense of true satisfaction or relief.

## Key Lessons

- **Prioritize worship and trust in Allah's provision**—spiritual devotion leads to inner peace and alleviation of worldly difficulties.

- **Neglect of worship results in the opposite**: a life filled with stress, problems, and unmet desires, with no true relief from poverty (physical or spiritual).

## 8.2 Daily Rituals and Their Transformative Power

Daily rituals in Islam, especially the five daily prayers (Salah), are central to shaping a Muslim's spiritual and personal life. These rituals are more than routine acts; they serve as powerful tools for fostering discipline, mindfulness, and spiritual connection.

### The Significance of the Five Daily Prayers (Salah)

Salah, one of the Five Pillars of Islam, is performed five times a day, serving as a continuous reminder of a Muslim's purpose and connection with the Creator. It is not just a ritualistic act but a direct communication channel with Allah, nurturing a deep spiritual bond. The Qur'an underscores the importance of Salah:

- "Indeed, prayer prohibits immorality and wrongdoing, and the remembrance of Allah is greater." (Quran, Al-Ankabut 29:45)

- "And establish prayer and give Zakat and bow with those who bow [in worship and obedience]." (Quran, Al-Baqarah 2:243)

- "Indeed, prayer has been decreed upon the believers a decree of specified times." (Quran, An-Nisa 4:103)

- "Certainly will the believers have succeeded: They who are during their prayer humbly submissive." (Quran, Al-Mu'minun 23:1-2)

Salah instills discipline, punctuality, and a structured daily routine in a Muslim. It fosters a continuous awareness of Allah, promoting mindfulness and spiritual consciousness.

## Cultivating Discipline, Mindfulness, and Spirituality Through Salah

Each prayer is an opportunity to step away from life's distractions, turn toward Allah, and reconnect with one's faith and purpose. This regular engagement nurtures a sense of closeness to Allah, emphasizing that He is the ultimate source of support, guidance, and mercy.

The structure and timing of Salah maintain a constant awareness of Allah throughout the day. From Fajr (pre-dawn) to Isha (night), the five prayers are spaced to keep a Muslim's heart and mind focused on divine consciousness. This consistent rhythm of worship prevents spiritual disconnection, reminding believers of their duties and offering a spiritual anchor amid daily life.

Salah is also an exercise in humility and submission. The physical acts of bowing and prostrating symbolize submission before Allah, recognizing His greatness and one's dependence on Him. This humility fosters spiritual discipline, reminding believers of their role in the universe and the necessity of relying on Allah.

Moreover, Salah shapes a Muslim's character and moral integrity. It encourages self-reflection, repentance, and striving for self-improvement. The repetition of Qur'anic verses during prayer reinforces key Islamic teachings—such as mercy, patience, and gratitude—helping shape a Muslim's ethical outlook.

## Spiritual Purification and Community Strength

Salah is a means of spiritual purification, allowing Muslims to seek forgiveness, ask for guidance, and express gratitude for Allah's blessings. This process cultivates a pure, humble heart that is aware of the need for divine mercy. It serves as a reminder that despite mistakes, Allah is always near, ready to forgive and guide.

The communal aspect of Salah strengthens the bonds within the Muslim community. While Salah can be performed individually, praying in a congregation, especially in a mosque, reinforces the sense of brotherhood and sisterhood, fosters unity, and cultivates a feeling of belonging to the Ummah (global Muslim community). This unity highlights that Muslims are part of a larger whole, bound by shared faith and devotion to Allah.

## The Transformative Power of Salah

Salah nurtures a profound spiritual connection with Allah. It is an expression of faith, a practice of discipline, and a means of spiritual purification. Muslims cultivate a constant awareness of Allah through Salah, strive for moral excellence, and maintain a deep relationship with the Creator. This regular practice keeps the heart spiritually grounded and empowers Muslims to face life's challenges with patience, resilience, and unwavering faith.

Performing Salah at designated times instills discipline and time management skills. The physical acts during Salah foster humility and submission, reinforcing the concept of servitude. Regular prayer encourages self-reflection, repentance, and gratitude—essential components of personal growth and spiritual development.

## 8.3 The Transformative Experience of Ramadan and Fasting (Sawm)

Fasting, or Sawm, during Ramadan, is one of the Five Pillars of Islam and plays a crucial role in spiritual development, self-discipline, and fostering empathy among Muslims.

"O you who have believed, decreed upon you is fasting as it was decreed upon those before you that you may become righteous – [Fasting for] a limited number of days. So whoever among you is ill or on a journey [during them] - then an equal number of days [are to be made up]. And upon those who are able [to fast, but with hardship] - a ransom [as substitute] of feeding a poor person [each day]. And whoever volunteers excess - it is better for him. But to fast is best for you, if you only knew. The month of Ramadhan [is that] in which the Qur'an was revealed, guidingexercise the people and clear proofs of guidance and criterion. So whoever sights [the new moon of] the month, let him fast it; and whoever is ill or on a journey - then an equal number of other days. Allah intends for you ease and does not intend for you hardship and [wants] for you to complete the period and to glorify Allah for that [to] which He has guided you, and perhaps you will be grateful." (Quran, Al-Baqarah 2:183-185)

Fasting during Ramadan goes beyond abstaining from food and drink; it involves refraining from all sinful behaviors, such as lying, backbiting, and arguing, from dawn until sunset. Through fasting, Muslims engage in an exercise of self-control, resisting physical desires as well as mental and emotional impulses. This conscious effort helps purify the soul, detach from worldly distractions, and deepen the spiritual connection with Allah.

## A Reminder of Human Fragility and Gratitude to Allah

Fasting is a powerful reminder of human fragility and reliance on Allah for sustenance. By willingly abstaining from basic needs, Muslims experience humility and acknowledge their dependence on the Creator. This realization fosters gratitude for Allah's blessings and encourages deeper spiritual awareness. Fasting helps cleanse the heart and mind of impurities, nurturing patience and cultivating inner peace and clarity. This purification is essential for spiritual growth, allowing believers to focus on worship, prayer, and reflection without daily distractions.

## Empathy, Compassion, and Community Solidarity

Fasting during Ramadan also cultivates empathy and compassion, especially for those less fortunate. By experiencing hunger and thirst, even temporarily, Muslims are reminded of the struggles faced by those who lack basic necessities. This shared experience enhances solidarity with the poor and underprivileged, inspiring acts of charity, generosity, and community support. It helps break down social barriers, fostering a sense of unity and equality as Muslims of all backgrounds partake in the fast together.

## Spiritual Reflection and Self-Improvement

Ramadan is a time for deep spiritual reflection and self-assessment. Muslims are encouraged to evaluate their actions and intentions, striving for spiritual and moral improvement. During this sacred month, Muslims read and reflect on the Qur'an, perform extra prayers (Taraweeh), and seek forgiveness for their sins. This heightened spirituality fosters closeness to Allah, increases good deeds, and inspires personal growth. Ramadan catalyzes positive change, motivating Muslims to adopt virtuous habits that extend beyond the fasting period.

## Strengthening Willpower and Resilience

Fasting is also an exercise in willpower and resilience. Abstaining from basic needs for an extended period demonstrates a high level of self-discipline and control. This discipline extends to other aspects of life, enabling Muslims to resist temptations that lead them away from their faith. The lessons learned during fasting help build strong character, enhance decision-making, and improve the ability to endure challenges.

## The Comprehensive Nature of Fasting

In essence, fasting during Ramadan is a multi-dimensional worship that extends beyond mere abstention from physical needs. It is a holistic spiritual exercise that purifies the soul, fosters empathy and compassion, strengthens community bonds, and encourages reflection and self-improvement. Through fasting, Muslims seek to draw closer to Allah, earn His pleasure and enhance their character, develop gratitude, and cultivate empathy for others. Fasting is a means of spiritual purification that transforms believers' inner and outer lives, making them more compassionate, disciplined, and spiritually conscious individuals.

## 8.4 The Impact of Charity on the Soul

Charity, both obligatory (Zakat) and voluntary (Sadaqah), is a core element of worship in Islam with profound effects on personal growth and spiritual development. It purifies one's wealth and soul, fosters empathy, and promotes social harmony.

### Transforming the Heart and Purifying the Soul Through Giving

Giving in charity transforms the heart by encouraging generosity, compassion, and responsibility toward others. The Qur'an encourages charity, stating:
"The example of those who spend their wealth in the way of Allah is like a seed [of grain] that sprouts seven ears; in every ear is a hundred grains. And Allah multiplies [His reward] for whom He wills." (Quran 2:261)

By giving a portion of one's wealth to those in need, Muslims purify their hearts from greed and attachment to material possessions. This selfless act cultivates empathy and solidarity with the less fortunate, aligning one's actions with the values of compassion and social justice.

### The Ripple Effect of Charity in Building a Compassionate Community

Charitable acts extend beyond the individual giver, contributing to a compassionate and cohesive community. The Prophet Muhammad (peace be upon him) said:
"The believer's shade on the Day of Resurrection will be his charity." (Sahih Tirmidhi)

This hadith emphasizes the significance of charity not only in this life but also in the Hereafter. Charity fosters unity, reduces social inequalities, and creates an environment where everyone is supported and cared for.

## Zakat: A Spiritual Practice Promoting Social Justice

Zakat, the obligatory form of charity, is more than a financial transaction; it is a profound spiritual practice that purifies one's wealth and soul while promoting social justice and compassion. The Qur'an repeatedly emphasizes its importance as one of the pillars of Islam:

"And establish prayer and give Zakat, and whatever good you put forward for yourselves - you will find it with Allah. Indeed, Allah of what you do, is Seeing." (Quran, Al-Baqarah 2:110)

"Take, [O Muhammad], from their wealth a charity by which you purify them and cause them to increase, and invoke [Allah's blessings] upon them. Indeed, your invocations are reassurance for them. And Allah is Hearing and Knowing." (Quran, At-Tawbah 9:103)

As one of the Five Pillars of Islam, Zakat requires Muslims to give a specific portion—usually 2.5% of their savings annually—to support those in need. This act teaches Muslims to detach from material wealth, cultivating humility and gratitude by reminding them that all wealth is a blessing from Allah and must be used in a way that pleases Him.

Zakat also fosters empathy and solidarity. By supporting the poor, orphans, widows, and others in need, Muslims are reminded of their responsibilities towards fellow human beings, helping to create a just and equitable society. The practice strengthens the sense of community (Ummah), where every individual's well-being is connected to others, promoting a culture of care and social responsibility.

## Sadaqah: The Spirit of Generosity and Voluntary Giving

Beyond Zakat, Islam encourages additional voluntary charity, known as Sadaqah. Unlike Zakat, which has a fixed amount, Sadaqah can be given at any time and in any amount, allowing Muslims to cultivate generosity continuously. Whether through financial support, sharing food, offering a kind word, or helping someone in need, Sadaqah encompasses various actions that benefit the community. This practice encourages a habit of selflessness and giving, nurturing a spirit of generosity in everyday life.

## Spiritual and Social Benefits of Charity

Whether through Zakat or Sadaqah, charity acts as a means of spiritual purification. It cleanses the heart of selfishness, arrogance, and attachment to material wealth, fostering humility and empathy. By recognizing the needs of others and striving to meet them, Muslims strengthen their faith and find greater purpose. Giving in charity becomes a way to draw closer to Allah, aligning one's actions with the values of compassion, justice, and mercy central to Islam.

On a social level, Zakat and Sadaqah help redistribute wealth, alleviate poverty, and reduce economic inequality. By ensuring wealth circulates rather than accumulates in a few's hands, these practices create a balanced society where everyone's basic needs are met. This economic stability fosters security and peace, enabling individuals and families to thrive and contribute positively to their community.

## Personal Stories of Transformation Through Charity

Many personal stories highlight the transformative power of charity in Islam. Muslims who engage in charitable activities often report increased fulfillment, inner peace, and spiritual growth. Acts of kindness, large or small, can transform both the giver and receiver, fostering gratitude, humility, and joy. These stories serve as a testament to charity's impact on personal development and community well-being.

## Charity as a Path to True Richness

In essence, Zakat and Sadaqah are more than financial obligations; they are acts of worship that nurture a generous spirit, foster empathy, and help Muslims grow spiritually by recognizing their interconnectedness with others. Through charity, Muslims purify their wealth and fulfill religious duties while cultivating a deeper understanding of true richness—being rich in piety, character, and a strong relationship with Allah. These practices encourage a life grounded in sharing, caring, and serving others for the sake of Allah, ultimately leading to greater fulfillment and a more meaningful existence.

## 8.5 Hajj (Pilgrimage) and Its Life-Changing Impact

Hajj, the pilgrimage to Mecca, is one of the Five Pillars of Islam and an essential act of worship for Muslims who are physically and financially able to undertake it at least once in their lifetime. Beyond being a physical journey, Hajj is a profound spiritual experience with the power to transform lives. It allows Muslims to renew their faith, seek forgiveness for their sins, and return to their daily lives with a renewed sense of purpose and spiritual clarity.

The Qur'an emphasizes the significance of Hajj:

- "And proclaim to the people the Hajj [pilgrimage]; they will come to you on foot and every lean camel; they will come from every distant pass." (Quran, Al-Hajj 22:27)

- "And [due] to Allah from the people is a pilgrimage to the House – for whoever is able to find thereto a way. But whoever disbelieves – then indeed, Allah is free from need of the worlds." (Quran, Ale Imran 3:97)

- "And complete the Hajj and 'Umrah for Allah. But if you are prevented, then [offer] what can be obtained with ease of sacrificial animals... And fear Allah and know that Allah is severe in penalty." (Quran, Al-Baqarah 2:196)

### Preparation: A Journey of Repentance and Readiness

The transformative effect of Hajj begins even before the journey itself. Preparing for Hajj requires physical, emotional, and spiritual readiness. Pilgrims are encouraged to make amends with others, settle debts, and seek forgiveness for wrongdoings. This preparation fosters humility and self-awareness, reminding Muslims of their mortality and the importance of repentance. The journey to Mecca serves as a reminder of the ultimate journey every human will undertake—returning to the Creator.

## The Rituals of Hajj: Symbols of Unity, Faith, and Submission

Once in Mecca, the rituals of Hajj deepen the transformative experience. Pilgrims perform a series of rites symbolizing unity among Muslims worldwide and their submission to Allah. The wearing of simple white garments, or Ihram, represents purity, equality, and the shedding of worldly distinctions such as wealth, status, and race. This reinforces the idea that all believers are equal in the eyes of Allah and true worth is measured by piety and devotion.

The ritual of Tawaf, or circling the Kaaba, symbolizes the unity of believers worshiping the One God, while Sa'i, the walking between the hills of Safa and Marwah, commemorates Hajar's desperate search for water for her son Isma'il, underscoring themes of perseverance, faith, and divine providence.

## Standing at Arafat: A Profound Moment of Spiritual Renewal

Standing at Arafat, also known as the "Day of Arafah," is perhaps the pinnacle of the Hajj experience. Pilgrims stand in earnest supplication, seeking Allah's mercy and forgiveness, reflecting on their lives, and resolving to make positive changes. This act of standing in prayer symbolizes the Day of Judgment, when all of humanity will stand before Allah. The collective gathering of millions of Muslims from all corners of the globe fosters a profound sense of global unity and brotherhood, reinforcing the belief that all Muslims are part of a single Ummah (community). This sense of unity often impacts pilgrims, inspiring them to return home with greater empathy, generosity, and responsibility toward others.

## Symbolic Acts of Sacrifice and Resisting Temptation

The conclusion of Hajj involves the symbolic stoning of the Jamarat, representing the rejection of evil and temptation, and the sacrifice of an animal, commemorating Prophet Ibrahim's (Abraham's) willingness to sacrifice his son in obedience to Allah. These acts are powerful reminders of obedience, sacrifice, and resisting temptation in one's spiritual journey. Pilgrims leave Hajj with a renewed sense of spiritual clarity and commitment, often experiencing profound changes in their priorities, values, and outlook on life.

## Lasting Effects of Hajj on Spirituality and Community

The impact of Hajj extends far beyond the pilgrimage itself. Many pilgrims describe a heightened sense of spirituality, inner peace, and a stronger commitment to their faith and community. Hajj serves as a spiritual reset, allowing Muslims to return to their daily lives with a clean slate and a renewed dedication to living according to Islamic principles. The transformative experience of Hajj is personal and has a ripple effect on families, communities, and societies, as pilgrims bring back a reinforced sense of faith, purpose, and commitment to doing good.

## Personal Stories of Transformation

Many Muslims who have completed Hajj share testimonies of profound spiritual transformation and renewal. They often describe feelings of spiritual rebirth, heightened awareness of Allah's presence, and a renewed commitment to their faith and community. The experience of Hajj leaves a lasting impact, inspiring greater devotion, humility, and a desire to lead a life reflecting Islamic principles.

## Hajj as a Path to Spiritual Rebirth

Hajj is a life-changing journey that encompasses deep spiritual reflection, communal worship, and a commitment to Allah. It purifies the soul, fosters unity, and inspires a renewed dedication to living by the principles of Islam. The transformative power of Hajj helps Muslims strengthen their relationship with Allah and become more compassionate, responsible, and spiritually aware individuals, deeply connected to their faith and community.

Worship in Islam is a powerful catalyst for personal growth and spiritual development. Acts of worship such as Salah, fasting, charity, and pilgrimage are not merely ritualistic practices; they are transformative experiences that foster discipline, empathy, humility, and a deep connection with Allah. This chapter has explored how these acts of worship contribute to personal development, enhance spiritual awareness, and transform an individual's character and conduct, leading to a more fulfilling and meaningful life.

The next chapter, "Social Transformation Through Islamic Values," will discuss how Islamic teachings promote social justice, compassion, and community building, contributing to a more just and equitable society.

# Chapter Nine

# Social Transformation Through Islamic Values

Islam is a religion of personal guidance and spiritual development and a comprehensive system that promotes social justice, equality, and community well-being. Its teachings encompass principles that, when implemented, transform individuals and societies. This chapter explores how Islamic values foster social transformation by promoting justice, compassion, and unity, creating a harmonious and equitable society.

## 9.1 The Role of Family and Community in Personal Growth

In Islam, the family is considered the cornerstone of society. A strong family structure fosters personal development, moral character, and social stability. Similarly, the wider community supports individual growth and nurtures a sense of belonging and responsibility.

### Islamic Teachings on the Importance of Family Ties and Social Bonds

Islam places great emphasis on maintaining strong family ties and fostering harmonious relationships. The Quran and Hadith provide numerous guidelines on the rights and responsibilities of family members. The Prophet Muhammad (peace be upon him) said: "The best of you are those who are best to their families." (Sunan Tirmidhi)

This Hadith highlights the importance of kindness, respect, and good conduct within the family. A stable and loving family environment provides a foundation for personal growth and instills values of empathy, patience, and cooperation.

## How Strong Family and Community Connections Support Individual Transformation

Strong family and community connections provide a supportive environment for personal transformation. Families offer emotional support, guidance, and encouragement, helping individuals navigate life's challenges. Likewise, the Muslim community, or Ummah, provides a network of support and accountability, encouraging members to uphold Islamic values and strive for personal excellence. This sense of belonging and collective responsibility fosters resilience and personal growth.

## Examples of Social Cohesion and Support Systems in Muslim Communities

Islamic teachings encourage the establishment of social support systems, such as charitable organizations, community centers, and educational institutions, which strengthen the community and support its members. Zakat (obligatory charity) and Sadaqah (voluntary charity) are key components of Islamic social welfare that promote social justice and equity. These initiatives help alleviate poverty, provide education, and support those in need, fostering a compassionate and cohesive society.

# 9.2 Islamic Principles of Social Justice and Equality

Islamic values strongly emphasize social justice, fairness, and equality. These principles are fundamental to Islamic teachings and provide a framework for creating a just and equitable society.

## The Quranic Emphasis on Justice, Fairness, and Equality

The Quran consistently calls for justice and fairness in all aspects of life. Allah commands: "O you who have believed, be persistently standing firm in justice, witnesses for Allah, even if it be against yourselves or parents and relatives." (Quran, An-Nisa 4:135)

This verse highlights the importance of upholding justice, even when it is difficult or goes against personal interests. Justice is considered a divine attribute and a central tenet of Islam, guiding social interactions, governance, and legal systems.

## How Islamic Teachings Can Transform Societies into Just and Equitable Places

Islamic teachings provide a comprehensive framework for social justice that addresses economic, political, and social inequalities. Principles such as fair trade, the prohibition of Riba (usury), and the equitable distribution of wealth through Zakat help reduce economic disparities and promote social welfare. Additionally, Islamic teachings on the rights of women, children, and minorities emphasize the importance of dignity, respect, and equal opportunities for all members of society.

## The Role of Muslims in Advocating for Social Justice in Contemporary Society

Muslims are encouraged to actively promote social justice and address societal injustices. The Prophet Muhammad (peace and blessings be upon him) said: "Whoever among you sees an evil action, let him change it with his hand [by taking action]; if he cannot, then with his tongue [by speaking out]; and if he cannot, then with his heart [by hating it], and that is the weakest of faith." (Sahih Muslim)

This Hadith underscores the importance of social activism and advocacy in Islam. Muslims are called to uphold justice, defend the oppressed, and work towards creating a more just and equitable society, both within their communities and in the broader world.

## 9.3 Promoting a Culture of Compassion and Kindness

Compassion and kindness are core values in Islam that contribute to transforming individuals and societies. By fostering a culture of empathy and mutual support, Islamic teachings promote social harmony and well-being.

### The Importance of Mercy and Compassion in Islam

Mercy and compassion are central to Islamic teachings, and Muslims are encouraged to embody these qualities in their interactions. The Prophet Muhammad (peace and blessings be upon him) said: "The merciful are shown mercy by the Most Merciful. Be merciful on the earth, and you will be shown mercy from above." (Sunan Tirmidhi)

This Hadith highlights the reciprocal nature of compassion and mercy. By showing kindness and empathy towards others, Muslims hope to receive Allah's mercy and blessings.

### Examples of How Islamic Values Promote a Caring and Inclusive Society

Islamic values encourage the development of a caring and inclusive society by promoting social welfare, protecting the rights of all individuals, and fostering a sense of community. Acts of charity, community service, and mutual aid are integral to Islamic practice, helping to build a supportive and compassionate environment where everyone is valued and cared for. For example, visiting the sick, supporting orphans, and providing for the needy emphasizes compassion and social responsibility in Islam.

## The Transformative Impact of Kindness on Both the Giver and the Receiver

Kindness has a transformative impact on both the giver and the receiver. For the giver, kindness fosters humility, gratitude, and a sense of fulfillment. For the receiver, they provide comfort, support, and a sense of belonging. The Quran encourages acts of kindness and reciprocity: "And whatever good you put forward for yourselves, you will find it with Allah. It is better and greater in reward." (Quran, Al-Muzzammil 73:20)

This verse emphasizes that Allah rewards every act of kindness, encouraging Muslims to contribute positively to their communities and the well-being of others.

Islamic values provide a powerful framework for social transformation, promoting justice, compassion, and community well-being. Islam encourages the development of a just and equitable society by emphasizing the importance of family and community ties, advocating for social justice and equality, and fostering a culture of kindness and empathy. This chapter has explored how Islamic teachings contribute to social transformation, highlighting the role of Muslims in building compassionate, inclusive communities that reflect the principles of Islam.

The next chapter, "Financial Ethics and Prosperity in Islam," will discuss how Islamic teachings guide financial practices, promote ethical wealth management, and foster economic justice, contributing to personal prosperity and social welfare.

# Mid Review Request Page

Dear Reader,

Thank you for embarking on the journey of **Islamic Transformation**. Your support and feedback mean a lot to me, and I hope this book has deepened your understanding and provided you with practical tools for personal growth. I would be truly grateful if you could take a few moments to share your thoughts about the book. Reviews play a vital role in helping others discover the guidance they may need for their own transformation, and your insights can make a real difference. Whether you share your review on Amazon, Goodreads, or any other platform, your honest feedback is greatly appreciated and will help spread this message far and wide.

Please click the link or scan the QR code below to submit your review.

https://www.amazon.com/review/review-your-purchases/?asin=B0DJR1BGWT

Again, Thank you for your support and for participating in this journey. May Allah reward you and bless you and your family in this life and the next. Aameen.

Your Sister in Islam

Aisha Othman

# Chapter Ten
# Financial Ethics and Prosperity in Islam

Islam provides a comprehensive framework for financial ethics encompassing fairness, justice, and responsibility principles. These teachings guide Muslims in managing their wealth in a way that is beneficial for themselves and society as a whole. Islamic financial principles foster personal prosperity and economic justice by promoting ethical wealth management, prohibiting exploitative practices, and encouraging generosity and social welfare. This chapter explores how these principles contribute to ethical financial behavior, economic stability, and social well-being.

## 10.1 The Islamic Perspective on Wealth and Prosperity

In Islam, wealth is viewed as a blessing from Allah and a means of fulfilling one's responsibilities toward oneself, one's family, and society. However, Islam emphasizes that wealth should be acquired, managed, and spent ethically.

**Understanding the Concept of Rizq (Provision) and Its Sources**

In Islamic teachings, Rizq refers to the sustenance or provision that Allah grants to His creation. The Quran states: "And there is no creature on earth but that upon Allah is its provision, and He knows its place of dwelling and place of storage." (Quran, Hud 11:6)

This verse highlights that Allah is the ultimate provider of all sustenance and decrees every creature's provision. This belief instills a sense of gratitude and reliance on Allah, encouraging Muslims to seek their Rizq through lawful (Halal) means and to trust Allah's wisdom and provision.

## The Balance Between Seeking Wealth and Maintaining Spiritual Priorities

While Islam encourages the pursuit of wealth through lawful means, it also warns against excessive attachment to material possessions. The Quran cautions: "Wealth and children are [but] adornment of the worldly life. But the enduring good deeds are better to your Lord for reward and better for [one's] hope." (Quran, Al-Kahf 18:46)

This verse reminds Muslims that while wealth is a part of worldly life, spiritual and ethical priorities should always take precedence. Maintaining a balance between seeking wealth and fulfilling spiritual obligations ensures that a Muslim's pursuit of prosperity does not lead to greed, dishonesty, or neglect of religious duties.

## How Islamic Financial Principles Can Lead to Ethical Prosperity

Islamic financial principles emphasize ethical behavior, fairness, and justice in all financial transactions. Prohibitions against exploitative practices such as Riba (usury) and Gharar (excessive uncertainty) ensure wealth is acquired and distributed fairly. By adhering to these principles, Muslims can achieve prosperity that is ethical, sustainable, and beneficial to society. Additionally, the concept of wealth as a trust from Allah encourages responsible management and generosity, fostering personal and communal well-being.

## 10.2 Implementing Fair Trade and Avoiding Riba (Usury)

Islamic teachings strongly advocate for fairness in trade and strictly prohibit exploitative practices such as Riba (usury), which can lead to economic injustice and exploitation.

### The Prohibition of Riba and Its Implications for Financial Ethics

Riba, or usury, is strictly prohibited in Islam due to its exploitative nature. The Quran explicitly forbids Riba: "Those who consume interest cannot stand [on the Day of Resurrection] except as one stand who Satan is beating into insanity. That is because they say, 'Trade is [just] like interest.' But Allah has permitted trade and has forbidden interest." (Quran, Al-Baqarah 2:275)

This prohibition is based on the principle that money should not be made from money without involving real economic activity or bearing some risk. Riba is considered exploitative because it takes advantage of those in need, leading to inequality and social injustice. By avoiding Riba, Muslims are encouraged to engage in fair trade and ethical financial practices that promote mutual benefit and economic justice.

### How Islamic Finance Promotes Fairness and Reduces Economic Inequality

Islamic finance promotes fairness by ensuring that all financial transactions are transparent, equitable, and based on economic activity. Concepts such as profit-sharing (Mudarabah) and joint ventures (Musharakah) encourage partnerships where both parties share profits and risks. This approach reduces economic inequality by preventing the concentration of wealth in the hands of a few and promoting broader participation in economic growth. Islamic finance also encourages ethical investing, where investments are made in industries and projects that are socially beneficial and do not harm the community.

## Personal Stories of Transformation Through Adopting Islamic Financial Practices

Many Muslims have experienced significant personal and financial growth by adopting Islamic financial practices. For example, individuals transitioning from conventional banking to Islamic banking often report a greater sense of ethical integrity, financial stability, and peace of mind. These personal stories illustrate the transformative impact of adhering to Islamic financial principles, demonstrating how ethical practices lead to personal prosperity and social welfare.

# 10.3 The Role of Zakat and Sadaqah in Wealth Redistribution

Zakat (obligatory charity) and Sadaqah (voluntary charity) are essential to Islamic financial ethics, which promote wealth redistribution and social welfare. These acts of charity purify wealth, support those in need, and foster a sense of community and solidarity.

## How Mandatory Almsgiving (Zakat) Helps Reduce Poverty and Build Stronger Communities

Zakat is one of the Five Pillars of Islam and is obligatory for all Muslims who meet the minimum wealth threshold (Nisab). It requires giving a fixed percentage (usually 2.5%) of one's accumulated wealth to specific categories of beneficiaries, such as the poor, the needy, and those in debt. The Quran emphasizes the importance of Zakat: "And establish prayer and give Zakat, and whatever good you put forward for yourselves – you will find it with Allah." (Quran, Al-Baqarah 2:110)

Zakat serves as a means of redistributing wealth and reducing economic disparities. By contributing to the welfare of those less fortunate, Muslims help build stronger, more cohesive communities. Zakat also purifies the giver's wealth and helps prevent excessive wealth accumulation in society.

## The Impact of Voluntary Charity (Sadaqah) on Personal Fulfillment and Social Harmony

In addition to Zakat, Islam encourages voluntary charity, known as Sadaqah. Unlike Zakat, Sadaqah is not obligatory and can be given in any amount and at any time. The Quran highlights the rewards of Sadaqah: "The example of those who spend their wealth in the way of Allah is like a seed [of grain] that sprouts seven ears; in every ear is a hundred grains. And Allah multiplies [His reward] for whom He wills." (Quran, Al-Baqarah 2:261)

Sadaqah fosters a spirit of generosity, compassion, and empathy, encouraging Muslims to support their communities and help those in need. Acts of voluntary charity promote social harmony and reduce feelings of envy and resentment, contributing to a more just and peaceful society.

## Examples of Successful Zakat Models and Their Transformative Effects on Society

Numerous successful Zakat models have significantly impacted society. Zakat funds support various social welfare programs in many Muslim-majority countries, such as education, healthcare, and poverty alleviation. These initiatives have helped improve living standards, reduce poverty, and promote economic stability. By implementing effective Zakat distribution models, communities can achieve greater social justice and economic equity, demonstrating the transformative potential of Islamic financial ethics.

Islamic financial ethics provide a comprehensive framework for managing wealth responsibly and ethically. By promoting fairness, justice, and generosity, Islam encourages ethical financial behavior that benefits individuals and society. Islamic teachings foster both personal prosperity and social welfare through the prohibition of exploitative practices like Riba, the encouragement of fair trade, and the promotion of wealth redistribution through Zakat and Sadaqah. This chapter has explored how these principles contribute to economic stability, ethical behavior, and social justice, creating a more equitable and prosperous society.

The next chapter, "Health, Wellness, and Islamic Practices," will explore how Islamic teachings promote physical health, mental well-being, and holistic wellness, providing a comprehensive approach to maintaining a balanced and healthy lifestyle.

# Chapter Eleven

# Health, Wellness, and Islamic Practices

Health and wellness are integral parts of Islamic teachings, which emphasize the importance of maintaining a balanced and healthy lifestyle. Islam provides comprehensive guidance on physical health, mental well-being, and spiritual wellness, recognizing that these aspects are interconnected and essential for holistic development. By adhering to Islamic principles related to diet, exercise, cleanliness, and mental health, Muslims can achieve a balanced state of well-being that promotes both physical vitality and spiritual fulfillment. This chapter explores how Islamic teachings foster a comprehensive approach to health and wellness.

## 11.1 The Importance of Physical Health in Islam

Islam encourages maintaining physical health as an essential component of overall well-being. The body is viewed as a trust from Allah, and Muslims are responsible for taking care of it through proper nutrition, exercise, and hygiene.

### The Prophet's Teachings on Maintaining Physical Health and Well-Being

The Prophet Muhammad (peace be upon him) emphasized the importance of maintaining good health and physical fitness. He encouraged Muslims to engage in physical activities and sports that promote strength and endurance. For example, he said: "The strong believer is better and more beloved to Allah than the weak believer, while there is good in both." (Sahih Muslim)

This Hadith highlights the importance of physical strength and vitality in fulfilling one's religious duties and serving the community. The Prophet also advocated for moderation in eating and drinking, emphasizing that overeating leads to physical ailments.

## How Physical Fitness and Good Nutrition Are Integral to Islamic Living

Physical fitness and good nutrition are integral to Islamic living because they contribute to a believer's overall health and effectiveness in fulfilling their religious and social responsibilities. The Quran encourages moderation and balance in consumption: "And eat and drink, but be not excessive. Indeed, He likes not those who commit excess." (Quran, An-'Am 7:31)

Following these guidelines, Muslims can maintain a healthy and balanced diet, avoid harmful habits, and promote physical fitness. Regular physical activity, such as walking, swimming, or engaging in sports, is encouraged to maintain a healthy body and prevent disease.

## Practical Tips for Adopting a Healthier Lifestyle According to Islamic Guidance

Adopting a healthier lifestyle by Islamic guidance involves several practical steps. These include consuming a balanced diet of fruits, vegetables, and whole grains, practicing portion control, staying hydrated, and avoiding harmful substances like alcohol and tobacco. Additionally, Muslims are encouraged to engage in regular physical activity, maintain good personal hygiene, and seek medical treatment when necessary. By incorporating these practices into daily routines, Muslims can maintain physical health and vitality.

## 11.2 Mental Health and Emotional Well-Being in Islam

Islamic teachings provide a holistic approach to mental and emotional well-being, recognizing the importance of maintaining a sound mind and physical health. The Quran and Hadith offer guidance on managing stress, anxiety, and other emotional challenges, emphasizing the role of faith and spirituality in achieving mental wellness.

### Understanding the Holistic Approach to Mental Health in Islamic Teachings

Islam recognizes the interconnectedness of the mind, body, and spirit, advocating for a balanced approach to mental health. The Quran provides comfort and guidance for those experiencing emotional distress, and the Prophet Muhammad (peace be upon him) offered practical advice for managing stress and anxiety. For instance, he recommended prayers and supplications (Du'a) to seek Allah's help and solace in difficult times.

"Verily, in the remembrance of Allah do hearts find rest." (Quran 13:28)

This verse highlights the calming effect of Dhikr (remembrance of Allah) on the mind and heart, emphasizing the importance of spiritual practices in achieving mental peace.

### Techniques for Maintaining Mental Well-Being Through Faith and Practice:**

Several techniques rooted in Islamic teachings can help maintain mental well-being. These include engaging in regular prayer (Salah), reciting the Quran, and performing Dhikr to cultivate a sense of calm and connection with Allah. Muslims are also encouraged to seek social support from family, friends, and the community, as social connections are vital for emotional well-being. Maintaining a positive mindset, practicing gratitude, and relying on Allah's wisdom and decree (Tawakkul) can help manage stress and anxiety.

## The Role of Community and Social Support in Managing Mental Health Issues

The Muslim community, or Ummah, plays a crucial role in supporting individuals facing mental health challenges. Islam encourages compassion, empathy, and mutual support among community members, providing a safety net for those experiencing emotional difficulties. The Prophet Muhammad (peace be upon him) said: "The example of the believers in their mutual love, mercy, and compassion is like that of a body: if one part of the body feels pain, the whole body responds with wakefulness and fever." (Sahih Bukhari and Muslim)

This Hadith underscores the importance of collective support and empathy within the community, emphasizing the need for Muslims to provide emotional and social support to those in need.

## 11.3 The Healing Power of Faith and Spiritual Practices

Islamic teachings highlight the healing power of faith and spiritual practices, which play a significant role in maintaining physical and mental health. Faith provides comfort, hope, and strength in times of adversity, while spiritual practices help maintain a balanced and harmonious state of being.

## The Spiritual and Psychological Benefits of Quranic Recitation and Prayer

Quranic recitation and prayer are powerful spiritual practices that provide numerous psychological benefits. The Quran is described as a source of healing and mercy: "And We send down of the Quran that which is healing and mercy for the believers..." (Quran, Al-Isra' 17:82)

Reciting the Quran and engaging in regular prayer can reduce stress, alleviate anxiety, and promote a sense of calm and peace. These practices help Muslims maintain a positive outlook, find solace in Allah's words, and develop a deeper connection with their Creator.

## How Faith Acts as a Source of Strength in Times of Illness and Hardship

Faith in Allah provides strength and resilience in times of illness and hardship. The belief that every trial is a test from Allah and that there is wisdom behind every difficulty helps Muslims cope with challenges with patience and hope. The Quran encourages seeking Allah's help through patience and prayer: "O you who have believed, seek help through patience and prayer. Indeed, Allah is with the patient." (Quran, Al-Baqarah 2:153)

This verse emphasizes the importance of relying on faith and prayer during difficult times, providing comfort and reassurance that Allah's support is always available.

## Personal Stories of Healing and Recovery Through Spiritual Means

Numerous personal stories illustrate the healing power of faith and spiritual practices in Islam. Many Muslims have found comfort and recovery from physical and mental ailments through sincere prayer, Quranic recitation, and trust in Allah's plan. These stories demonstrate the transformative impact of faith on health and wellness, highlighting how spiritual practices can promote healing and provide strength during times of adversity.

Islamic teachings provide a holistic approach to health and wellness, encompassing physical, mental, and spiritual wellness. By adhering to principles related to diet, exercise, cleanliness, and mental health, Muslims can achieve a balanced state of well-being that promotes physical vitality and spiritual fulfillment. This chapter has explored how Islamic teachings foster a comprehensive approach to health and wellness, highlighting the importance of maintaining a balanced and healthy lifestyle for overall well-being.

The next chapter will explore how kindness to parents can transform one's life on multiple levels, both internally and externally.

# Chapter Twelve

# The Power of Kindness to Parents in Islamic Personal Growth

The journey of personal transformation in Islam is deeply rooted in cultivating righteous character and fulfilling obligations to others. Being kind and dutiful to one's parents is at the forefront of these obligations. This duty is not merely a familial obligation but a profound spiritual practice that can transform one's life on multiple levels, both internally and externally.

## 12.1 The Pleasure of Parents is the Pleasure of Allah

First and foremost, the concept of being kind and dutiful to parents is directly linked to seeking the pleasure of Allah. The Quran and the Sunnah consistently emphasize the value of this kindness, often placing it immediately after the command to worship Allah alone. By aligning one's actions with this divine command, one earns Allah's pleasure and experiences a transformation in the heart—developing humility, gratitude, and a sense of selflessness. These qualities are essential to the Islamic process of personal growth, as they help purify the soul and draw closer to Allah.

The Prophet Muhammad (peace and blessings be upon him) said: "The pleasure of Allah lies in the pleasure of the father, and the displeasure of Allah lies in the displeasure of the father." [Jami` at-Tirmidhi 1899]

This hadith underscores the profound connection between being dutiful and pleasing to one's parents and attaining the pleasure of Allah. It emphasizes that treating parents with kindness, respect, and consideration is a moral duty and an essential aspect of one's spiritual success.

The Prophet Muhammad (peace and blessings be upon him) also said: "May he be humbled, may he be humbled, may he be humbled." It was said: "Who, O Messenger of Allah?" He said: "Whoever lives to see his parents in their old age, one or both of them and does not enter Paradise (by being dutiful to them)." [Sahih Muslim 2551]

"The father is the middle of the gates of Paradise, so keep to this gate or lose it." [Sunan Ibn Majah 3663]

It is also reported that the Prophet (peace and blessings be upon him) said: "Whoever comes into the morning and both his parents are pleased with him, he comes into the morning with two doors of Paradise open to him. Whoever goes into the evening and both parents are pleased with him goes into the evening with two doors of Paradise open for him. And if he has just one parent, then one door of Paradise is open to him. Whoever comes into the morning and his parents are angry with him comes in the morning with 2 doors of hellfire open. Whoever goes into the evening with both parents are angry with him, he goes into the evening with 2 doors of hellfire open to him. And if he has just one parent, then one door is open for him." After realizing this huge position of parents that the Prophet (peace and blessings be upon him) was telling the companions about, one of the Companions asked, "Even if the parents were oppressive to them?" The Prophet, Allah bless him and grant him peace, replied, "Even if they oppress the child, even if they oppress the child, even if they oppress the child."

These hadiths highlight that treating parents well and gaining their pleasure opens the gate to Paradise, implying a special favor from Allah for those who maintain good relationships with their parents.

## 12.2 Developing Empathy and Emotional Intelligence Through Being Dutiful to Parents

Being dutiful to parents also plays a transformative role in developing empathy and emotional intelligence. Caring for parents, particularly in times of their old age or vulnerability, requires patience, understanding, and compassion. Through this experience, one learns to put the needs of others before their own and to approach life's challenges with a nurturing attitude. Such an attitude extends beyond the family and influences how one interacts with the broader community, transforming relationships at every level and fostering a spirit of unity and mutual respect.

Moreover, honoring parents brings blessings into one's life. Parents' prayers and good wishes are powerful means of attaining barakah (blessings) in all aspects of life—career, relationships, or personal endeavors. When children fulfill their responsibilities towards their parents, they often find their lives enriched with peace and contentment. This spiritual and emotional fulfillment lays a strong foundation for transforming one's character and achieving a life that is both meaningful and aligned with the principles of Islam.

## 12.3 Dutiful to Parents Teaches Consistency in Action

On a practical level, being dutiful to parents teaches consistency in action, which is a cornerstone of personal transformation. Just as personal growth in Islam is achieved through small, consistent actions over time, being kind to parents requires ongoing effort. It involves regular communication, acts of service, and expressions of love and gratitude. These consistent actions help build a disciplined character, teaching the value of sustained effort and devotion, which can be applied to all other areas of life.

Additionally, caring for one's parents provides a powerful reminder of the cyclical nature of human life—the care they provide in our childhood is returned to them in their later years. Recognizing this cycle helps one develop a sense of purpose and belonging, understanding their role in a broader context of family and community. This perspective is crucial for anyone seeking transformation, as it encourages one to move beyond a self-centered view of life, embracing their role in a chain of nurturing and support that spans generations.

## 12.4 Kindness to Parents Reflects Relationship with Allah

Ultimately, the kindness shown to parents reflects one's relationship with Allah and commitment to embodying Islamic values. Through this act, a person not only fulfills their religious obligations but also embarks on a journey of inner transformation—nurturing the qualities of gratitude, humility, compassion, and steadfastness. These qualities are a building block for creating a better version of oneself, continuously striving towards higher spiritual ideals, one small, consistent change at a time.

The Quran consistently emphasizes the importance of being dutiful and kind to parents, highlighting gratitude, care, and humility toward them, especially in old age.

- "And your Lord has decreed that you not worship except Him, and to parents, good treatment. Whether one
or both of them reach old age [while] with you, say not to them [so much as], "uff," and do not repel them but speak to them a noble word." [Quran, al-Isra' 17:23]

- "And We have enjoined upon man [care] for his parents. His mother carried him, [increasing her] in weakness upon
weakness, and his weaning is in two years. Be grateful to Me and your parents; to Me is the [final] destination. But if they endeavor to make you associate with Me that of which you do not know, do not obey them but accompany them in [this] world with appropriate kindness and follow the way of those who turn back to Me [in repentance]. Then to Me will be your return, and I will inform you about what you used to do." [Quran, Luqman 31:14-15]

- "And We have enjoined upon man goodness to parents. But if they endeavor to make you associate with Me that of which you do not know, do not obey them. To Me is your return, and I will inform you about what you used to do." [Quran, Al-Ankabut 29:8]

- 'And We have enjoined upon man, to his parents, good treatment. His mother carried him with hardship and gave birth to him with hardship, and his gestation and weaning [period] is thirty months. [He grows] until, when he reaches maturity and reaches [the age of] forty years, he says, "My Lord, enable me to be grateful for Your favor which You have bestowed upon me and my parents and to work righteousness of which You will approve and make
righteous for me my offspring. Indeed, I have repented to You, and indeed, I am of the Muslims."' [Quran, Al-Ahqaf 46:15]

- 'And [recall] when We took the covenant from the Children of Israel, [enjoining upon them], "Do not worship except Allah, and to parents do good and to relatives, orphans, and the needy. And speak to people good [words], establish prayer, and give zakah." Then you turned away, except a few of you, and you were refusing.'[Quran, Al Baqarah 2:83]

- "Worship Allah and associate nothing with Him, and to parents do good, and to relatives, orphans, the needy, the near neighbor, the neighbor farther away, the companion at your side, the traveler, and those your right hands possess. Indeed, Allah does not like those who are self-deluding and boastful." [Quran, An-Nisa 4:36]

## 12.5 Understanding Why Some Children are Not Dutiful Kind to Their Parents

Despite the clear Quranic guidance emphasizing kindness and respect towards parents, many children may not heed these commands due to social, psychological, cultural, and individual factors. Here are some reasons why this may happen:

## Changing Social Values

In modern societies, individualism and personal autonomy are often highly valued. These values can sometimes conflict with the traditional expectations of family responsibilities, leading some children to
prioritize their independence over caring for their parents.

## Generational Differences

Generational gaps in perspectives, values, and experiences can lead to misunderstandings and conflicts between parents and children. Technological advancements and societal changes can create differences that make it difficult for children to relate to their parents' worldview.

## Lack of Religious Awareness

Many children may not have a strong understanding of or connection to their faith, resulting in a lack of awareness or appreciation of the Islamic teachings on being good to parents. This can happen if religious education is not prioritized or the family environment does not foster a deep understanding of these values.

## Negative Experiences

Sometimes, children may have experienced difficult or even traumatic relationships with their parents. In cases where parents have been abusive, overly controlling, or neglectful, children may find it emotionally challenging to follow these commands despite the teachings.

## Cultural Norms and Influences

In some cultures, emphasis on individual success, career, or lifestyle can lead to children placing their personal ambitions above their responsibilities to their parents. The influence of peer groups and media can also promote lifestyles that do not align with family care and respect for parents.

## Miscommunication or Lack of Emotional Bond

Poor communication or lack of an emotional bond can make it hard for children to fulfill their duties towards parents. If children do not feel a close connection or understanding, they may become distant and neglect their responsibilities.

## Economic Pressures

In some cases, economic pressures can create tension. Children struggling to manage their careers, finances, or their own families might feel overwhelmed, making it difficult to provide the level of support their parents need.

## Influence of Modern Lifestyles

The fast-paced nature of modern life and the influence of social media and technology can sometimes lead to children becoming more self-centered or distracted. The hustle culture often means less time is dedicated to relationships, including that with parents.

## Lack of Positive Role Models

It may not be their priority if children do not see positive examples of caring for parents in their environment. Seeing others, including extended family or friends, neglecting their responsibilities towards their parents can normalize such behavior.

## Emotional Detachment in Upbringing

If parents do not foster a loving, nurturing environment while raising their children, the bond required for later care and kindness may be weak. Emotional detachment in upbringing can hinder the natural inclination towards showing gratitude and care.

To address these issues, a holistic approach is needed. Strengthening religious education, fostering emotional bonds from an early age, addressing generational differences with empathy, and creating a culture of respect and care for elders are all steps that can help bridge this gap. A conscious effort towards understanding the value of parents and making family responsibilities a priority can foster a more balanced approach to fulfilling these Quranic commands.

The next chapter, "Relationships and Community Building," will explore how Islamic teachings guide relationships within the family and the wider community, emphasizing the importance of strong social bonds, mutual support, and communal harmony in fostering personal and social growth.

# Chapter Thirteen
# Relationships and Community Building

Islam places a strong emphasis on the importance of relationships and community. The teachings of Islam provide comprehensive guidance on maintaining healthy relationships within the family and the wider community, emphasizing principles such as mutual respect, compassion, cooperation, and support. Strong social bonds and a sense of belonging are vital for personal growth and social harmony. This chapter explores how Islamic teachings guide family and community relationships, promote community building, and foster a sense of unity and solidarity among Muslims.

## 13.1 Building Strong Marriages and Family Bonds

The family is considered the cornerstone of Islamic society. Strong family bonds are essential for fostering personal development, moral character, and social stability. Islam provides detailed guidance on maintaining healthy and harmonious family relationships.

### The Role of Mutual Respect, Love, and Understanding in Islamic Marriages

Marriage in Islam is regarded as a sacred bond and a partnership based on mutual respect, love, and understanding. The Quran emphasizes the importance of love and mercy between spouses: "And among His signs is this: that He created for you mates from among yourselves, that you may dwell in tranquility with them, and He has put love and mercy between your (hearts)." (Quran, Ar-Rum 30:21)

This verse highlights the significance of compassion and understanding in a marital relationship. Both spouses are encouraged to treat each other with kindness, fulfill each other's rights, and support one another in fulfilling their religious and worldly responsibilities.

## Parenting According to Islamic Principles: Raising Righteous Children

Parenting is a significant responsibility in Islam, as parents are entrusted with the duty of raising righteous children who will grow up to be morally upright and responsible members of society. The Prophet Muhammad (peace be upon him) emphasized the importance of good upbringing: "Every one of you is a shepherd, and every one of you is responsible for his flock." (Sahih Bukhari)

Islamic parenting involves providing not only for the physical and educational needs of children but also nurturing their spiritual development. Parents are encouraged to teach their children the principles of Islam, model good behavior, and instill values such as honesty, integrity, and compassion from an early age.

## How Strong Family Bonds Foster Personal and Spiritual Growth

Strong family bonds provide a supportive environment for personal and spiritual growth. A stable and loving family environment fosters a sense of security and belonging, essential for emotional well-being. Family members support one another in practicing their faith, encourage personal development, and provide guidance and advice in times of difficulty. The family serves as a microcosm of the wider Muslim community, reflecting the principles of cooperation, support, and unity.

## 13.2 Strengthening Community Ties and Building a Supportive Ummah

The concept of Ummah, or the global Muslim community, is central to Islamic teachings. Islam encourages Muslims to build strong community ties, support one another, and work together towards common goals. A cohesive and supportive community is essential for promoting social harmony and collective well-being.

### The Importance of Brotherhood and Sisterhood in Islam

Islam teaches that all Muslims are brothers and sisters in faith, regardless of their race, nationality, or social status. The Prophet Muhammad (peace be upon him) said: "The believers, in their mutual kindness, compassion, and sympathy, are just like one body. When one of the limbs suffers, the whole body responds to it with wakefulness and fever." (Sahih Bukhari and Muslim)

This Hadith emphasizes the importance of solidarity and empathy within the Muslim community. Muslims are encouraged to support one another, share in each other's joys and sorrows, and work together to build a stronger and more cohesive community.

### How Islamic Teachings Promote Community Service and Volunteering

Community service and volunteering are highly encouraged in Islam as acts of worship and expressions of social responsibility. Muslims are urged to help those in need, support charitable causes, and contribute to the well-being of their communities. The Quran states: "The example of those who spend their wealth in the way of Allah is like a seed [of grain] that sprouts seven ears; in every ear is a hundred grains. And Allah multiplies [His reward] for whom He wills." (Quran, Al-Baqarah 2:261)

This verse highlights the immense rewards for those who engage in charitable acts and contribute to community welfare. Community service helps build a sense of unity and fosters a spirit of cooperation and mutual support.

## Creating Inclusive and Supportive Community Spaces

Islamic teachings encourage the creation of inclusive and supportive community spaces where all members feel welcome and valued. Mosques, community centers, and Islamic organizations play a crucial role in fostering a sense of belonging and providing support services, such as educational programs, counseling, and social activities. These spaces serve as hubs for community building, where Muslims can come together to worship, learn, and support one another in their personal and spiritual journeys.

## 13.3 Conflict Resolution and Promoting Social Harmony

Islam guides resolving conflicts and promoting social harmony within families and communities. Muslims can address disputes and foster a peaceful and cohesive environment by adhering to principles of justice, fairness, and compassion.

### Islamic Principles for Resolving Conflicts Within Families and Communities

Conflict is a natural part of human interactions, but Islam provides clear guidance on resolving disputes just and fairly. The Quran advises: "And if two groups of believers fight, then make peace between them. But if one of them oppresses the other, then fight against the one that oppresses until it returns to the ordinance of Allah. And if it returns, then make peace between them in justice and act justly. Indeed, Allah loves those who act justly." (Quran, Al-Hujurat 49:9)

This verse emphasizes the importance of justice and fairness in conflict resolution. Muslims are encouraged to seek peaceful solutions, mediate disputes, and uphold the principles of justice and equity in resolving conflicts within families and communities.

## Promoting Forgiveness and Reconciliation

Forgiveness and reconciliation are highly valued in Islam as a means of promoting social harmony and unity. The Quran encourages forgiveness: "But if you pardon and overlook and forgive - then indeed, Allah is Forgiving and Merciful." (Quran, At-Taghabun 64:14)

Muslims are urged to forgive others, overlook their faults, and seek reconciliation whenever possible. Forgiveness is a sign of strength and compassion, contributing to a peaceful and harmonious society.

## The Role of Compassion and Empathy in Fostering a Harmonious Community

Compassion and empathy are essential qualities for fostering a harmonious community. The Prophet Muhammad (peace be upon him) demonstrated these qualities in his interactions with others, always seeking to understand their perspectives and showing kindness and understanding. By practicing compassion and empathy, Muslims can build stronger, more supportive communities where everyone feels valued and respected.

Islamic teachings provide comprehensive guidance on maintaining healthy relationships and building strong communities. Islam fosters strong family bonds and cohesive communities that support personal and social growth by emphasizing the importance of mutual respect, compassion, and cooperation. This chapter has explored how Islamic principles guide relationships within the family and the wider community, promote community building, and foster a sense of unity and solidarity among Muslims, contributing to social harmony and collective well-being.

The next chapter, "Overcoming Challenges and Striving for Excellence," will explore how Islamic teachings encourage resilience, perseverance, and striving for excellence in all aspects of life, providing guidance on overcoming challenges and achieving personal and spiritual growth.

# Chapter Fourteen

# Overcoming Challenges and Striving for Excellence

Life is filled with challenges and trials, but Islam provides a framework for overcoming these difficulties with faith, resilience, and determination. Islamic teachings encourage believers to strive for excellence (Ihsan) in all aspects of life, embracing hardships as opportunities for growth and self-improvement. This chapter explores how Islam fosters resilience, perseverance, and a commitment to excellence, offering guidance on navigating life's challenges while maintaining spiritual and personal integrity.

## 14.1 The Islamic Perspective on Challenges and Trials

In Islam, challenges and trials are viewed as tests from Allah, designed to strengthen a believer's faith and character. These tests are opportunities for personal growth, purification, and spiritual development.

### Understanding the Concept of Trials as Tests from Allah

The Quran repeatedly mentions that life is a test, with good and bad experiences as opportunities to demonstrate faith and reliance on Allah. Allah says: "Do people think that they will be left alone because they say: 'We believe,' and will not be tested?" (Quran, Al-Amkabut 29:2)

This verse highlights that every believer will face tests in their life, and these trials are part of Allah's divine plan to purify and elevate their faith. Understanding that challenges are divinely ordained tests helps Muslims maintain perspective and develop a sense of resilience and trust in Allah's wisdom.

## Embracing Hardships as Opportunities for Spiritual Growth

Islam teaches that hardships and difficulties can lead to spiritual growth and a closer relationship with Allah. The Prophet Muhammad (peace be upon him) said: "The greatest reward comes with the greatest trial. When Allah loves a people, He tests them; whoever accepts that wins His pleasure, but whoever is discontent with that earns His wrath." (Sunan Ibn Majah)

This Hadith emphasizes that trials are a means of attaining Allah's pleasure and reward. By embracing hardships with patience (Sabr) and gratitude (Shukr), Muslims can grow spiritually, strengthen their faith, and develop a deeper trust in Allah's wisdom and mercy.

## How Islamic Teachings Encourage a Positive Attitude Toward Challenges

Islamic teachings encourage a positive attitude toward challenges, emphasizing patience, perseverance, and reliance on Allah. The Quran provides reassurance: "So, verily, with hardship, there is relief. Verily, with hardship, there is relief." (Quran, Ash-Sharh 94:5-6)

These verses remind believers that every hardship is accompanied by relief and that Allah's mercy and assistance are always near. By maintaining a positive outlook and trusting Allah's plan, Muslims can navigate challenges with resilience and hope.

## 14.2 Developing Resilience and Perseverance

Resilience and perseverance are key qualities that Islam encourages when facing life's challenges. By cultivating these attributes, Muslims can overcome adversity and achieve their goals while remaining steadfast in their faith.

### The Importance of Sabr (Patience) in Facing Adversity

Sabr, or patience, is a fundamental virtue in Islam that helps believers remain steadfast in adversity. The Quran emphasizes the importance of patience: "O you who have believed, seek help through patience and prayer. Indeed, Allah is with the patient." (Quran, Al-Baqarah 2:153)

Patience involves enduring difficulties without complaint, maintaining faith in Allah's wisdom, and trusting that every hardship serves a greater purpose. It is an active state of resilience that requires strength, self-control, and perseverance.

### Strategies for Cultivating Perseverance and Strength of Character

Cultivating perseverance and strength of character involves developing a mindset of resilience, embracing challenges as opportunities for growth, and seeking support from Allah and the community. Practical strategies include engaging in regular prayer (Salah), seeking guidance from the Quran, and remembering the examples of the Prophets and righteous predecessors who demonstrated remarkable perseverance in the face of trials. Additionally, surrounding oneself with supportive, like-minded individuals and seeking counsel from knowledgeable and experienced mentors can help reinforce resilience and perseverance.

## Learning from the Lives of the Prophets and Companions Who Overcame Great Trials

The lives of the Prophets and companions provide powerful examples of resilience and perseverance in the face of great trials. For instance, the Prophet Ayyub (Job) demonstrated extraordinary patience and faith during his illness and loss. The Prophet Muhammad (peace be upon him) himself endured numerous hardships, including persecution, exile, and personal loss, yet remained steadfast in his mission and commitment to Allah. These examples inspire and guide Muslims, illustrating how faith and perseverance can help overcome difficult challenges.

## 14.3 Striving for Excellence (Ihsan) in All Aspects of Life

Islam encourages striving for excellence, or Ihsan, in every aspect of life. Ihsan means doing one's best, not only in worship but also in one's personal, professional, and social endeavors.

### The Concept of Ihsan and Its Application to Daily Life

Ihsan is the highest level of faith and worship, characterized by performing every action with sincerity, devotion, and excellence. The Prophet Muhammad (peace be upon him) explained: "Ihsan is to worship Allah as if you see Him, and if you do not see Him, then [know that] He sees you." (Sahih Muslim)

This Hadith emphasizes the importance of mindfulness and sincerity in all actions. By striving for Ihsan, Muslims are encouraged to perform every task to the best of their abilities, whether worship, work, or interacting with others.

## How to Apply the Principle of Ihsan in Personal and Professional Endeavors

Applying the principle of Ihsan involves setting high standards for oneself in every aspect of life. In personal endeavors, it means being sincere in worship, maintaining honesty and integrity, and striving to improve oneself continually. Professional endeavors involve pursuing excellence in one's work, being ethical and fair in business dealings, and contributing positively to one's community and society. Muslims can achieve personal growth, professional success, and spiritual fulfillment by embodying Ihsan.

## Examples of Excellence in Islamic History and Contemporary Society

Islamic history is filled with examples of individuals who embodied Ihsan in their lives, achieving greatness through their dedication to excellence. Scholars like Imam Al-Ghazali and Ibn Sina (Avicenna) excelled in their fields while remaining deeply committed to their faith. Contemporary examples include Muslims who have succeeded in various professions, such as medicine, law, academia, and entrepreneurship, by adhering to Islamic values and striving for excellence. These meaningful role models demonstrate how Ihsan can lead to worldly success and spiritual fulfillment.

## 14.4 Navigating Modern Challenges with Faith and Integrity

The modern world presents unique challenges that require a balanced approach guided by faith and integrity. Islam provides tools and principles for navigating these challenges while maintaining a commitment to Islamic values.

## Balancing Faith and Modernity

Muslims today face the challenge of balancing their faith with the demands of modern life. This balance requires a deep understanding of Islamic teachings and the ability to apply them in a contemporary context. The Quran and Sunnah provide timeless guidance that can be adapted to modern challenges, ensuring that Muslims remain true to their values while engaging with the world meaningfully.

## Addressing Social and Ethical Challenges

Modern society faces various social and ethical challenges, including economic inequality, environmental degradation, and social justice issues. Islam urges Muslims to uphold integrity and actively engage in addressing these challenges despite the pressures of today's fast-paced and materialistic world. Islam promotes justice, fairness, and compassion, encouraging Muslims to use their skills and resources to contribute positively to society. By advocating for ethical practices and working toward a more just and equitable world, Muslims can help foster a society grounded in moral values.

## Maintaining Integrity in the Face of Temptations and Pressures

Maintaining integrity can be challenging in today's fast-paced and often materialistic world. Islamic teachings emphasize the importance of honesty, trustworthiness, and ethical conduct, even in the face of temptation and pressure. Muslims are encouraged to seek strength through prayer, community support, and reliance on Allah, ensuring they uphold their principles and values regardless of external circumstances.

Islam provides a comprehensive framework for overcoming challenges and striving for excellence in all aspects of life. By cultivating resilience, perseverance, and a commitment to Ihsan, Muslims can navigate life's difficulties with faith and integrity, achieving personal and spiritual growth. This chapter has explored how Islamic teachings encourage a positive attitude toward challenges, promote resilience and perseverance, and inspire a commitment to excellence, providing a roadmap for achieving success and fulfillment in this life and the Hereafter.

# Chapter Fifteen

# Preparing for the Hereafter

In Islamic teachings, life in this world is viewed as a temporary journey, a preparation for the eternal life that follows. The belief in the Hereafter, or life after death, is fundamental to the Islamic faith. This chapter will explore how the belief in the Hereafter shapes a Muslim's approach to life, influences their actions, and motivates them to live with a sense of purpose, accountability, and hope.

## 15.1 Belief in the Afterlife

The concept of the Hereafter is central to Islamic belief, underscoring the idea that this worldly life is transient and that the ultimate goal is to attain success in the life to come. The Qur'an repeatedly reminds believers of the reality of the Hereafter, where every soul will be judged for its deeds and rewarded or punished accordingly.

The belief in an afterlife provides a broader perspective on existence, urging individuals to reflect on the impermanence of this world. It encourages Muslims to focus on immediate gains and actions that will bring lasting rewards in the Hereafter. This mindset fundamentally transforms how Muslims approach life, driving them to make choices that align with divine guidance and ethical principles.

In Surah Al-Baqarah, Allah says: "This is the Book about which there is no doubt, a guidance for those conscious of Allah – Who believe in the unseen, establish prayer, and spend out of what We have provided for them." (Qur'an, Al-Baqarah 2:2-3)

The phrase "believe in the unseen" includes belief in the Hereafter, where all actions will be accounted for. This belief fosters a sense of accountability, knowing that every deed, whether seen or unseen, will be judged by Allah.

## 15.2 Prioritizing the Hereafter

Anas bin Malik narrated that the Messenger of Allah (peace and blessings be upon him) said:"Whoever makes the Hereafter his goal, Allah makes his heart rich, and organizes his affairs, and the world comes to him whether it wants to or not. And whoever makes the world his goal, Allah puts his poverty right before his eyes, and disorganizes his affairs, and the world does not come to him, except what has been decreed for him." (At-Tirmidhi and Ibn Majah)

**Focus on the Hereafter**

The hadith emphasizes the importance of making the Hereafter (the eternal life after death) one's primary goal. When a person is focused on pleasing Allah and striving for the rewards of the Hereafter, Allah grants them inner contentment and peace of mind and takes care of their worldly affairs. The person is not distracted by the material world, and yet, Allah provides for them without them having to chase worldly gains excessively.

**Pursuing Worldly Matters Alone**

Conversely, when someone focuses solely on the material world (wealth, status, or desires), Allah places poverty before their eyes. This means that despite accumulating wealth or possessions, such a person will feel unsatisfied and always fear losing what they have. Their life becomes filled with stress and disorder, and they may never attain the full worldly gains they desire except for what is already destined for them.

**Lesson – Balance and Prioritization:**

This hadith teaches that when a person prioritizes the Hereafter, Allah blesses both their spiritual and worldly lives. However, chasing the world without regard for Allah and the Hereafter leads to inner turmoil and unfulfilled desires.

## 15.3 Living with a Higher Purpose

The awareness of eternal life beyond this temporary world encourages Muslims to live with a higher purpose. Islam teaches that every moment of this worldly life is an opportunity to earn Allah's pleasure and prepare for the Hereafter. When performed with the right intention, everyday activities, even mundane tasks, transform into acts of worship.

For instance, providing for one's family, helping a neighbor, or even smiling at someone can be considered acts of charity if done to seek Allah's pleasure. This mindset encourages believers to infuse their lives with purpose, striving to align their actions with the values of compassion, justice, and righteousness.

The Prophet Muhammad (peace be upon him) emphasized this principle in a hadith: "The believer's affair is all good, and this applies only to a believer. If something good happens to him, he thanks Allah, which is good for him. If something bad happens to him, he bears it patiently, which is also good for him." (Sahih Muslim)

This hadith illustrates the comprehensive nature of Islam's guidance, showing how a believer's life is constantly oriented towards a higher purpose, whether in times of ease or difficulty.

## 15.4 Continuous Self-Reflection and Repentance

An essential aspect of preparing for the Hereafter is continuous self-reflection and seeking repentance. Islam teaches that humans are inherently fallible and prone to mistakes and sins. However, it also emphasizes Allah's boundless mercy and the importance of repentance.

The act of repentance, or *Tawbah*, is a powerful tool for spiritual cleansing and transformation. It allows believers to acknowledge their mistakes, seek forgiveness, and strive to improve. Repentance is not just about feeling remorse; it also involves a sincere intention to turn away from the sin and make amends where possible.

Allah says in the Qur'an: "And those who, when they commit an immorality or wrong themselves [by transgression], remember Allah and seek forgiveness for their sins – and who can forgive sins except Allah? – and [who] do not persist in what they have done while they know." (Qur'an, AleImran 3:135)

This ayah highlights the importance of being mindful of one's actions and turning back to Allah in sincere repentance whenever one falls short. It also reassures believers that Allah's forgiveness is always within reach, no matter how grave the sin, as long as they are willing to repent sincerely.

## 15.5 Aligning Worldly Actions with Eternal Goals

The belief in the Hereafter fundamentally influences how Muslims view their actions in this world. It encourages a mindset where every deed is weighed not just for its immediate benefits but also for its impact on the Hereafter. This perspective fosters a holistic approach to life, where spiritual and material pursuits are balanced and interwoven.

For example, while Islam encourages earning a lawful livelihood and enjoying the bounties of life, it also warns against excessive attachment to worldly pleasures. The Qur'an provides numerous reminders of this world's transient nature and the importance of prioritizing the eternal over the temporary.

Allah says: "Know that the life of this world is but amusement and diversion and adornment and boasting to one another and competition in increase of wealth and children – like the example of a rain whose [resulting] plant growth pleases the tillers; then it dries, and you see it turned yellow; then it becomes [scattered] debris. And in the Hereafter is severe punishment and forgiveness from Allah and approval. And what is the worldly life except the enjoyment of delusion." (Qur'an, Al-Hadid 57:20)

This ayah encourages believers to maintain a balanced perspective, recognize the fleeting nature of worldly life, and focus on what will bring them closer to Allah and eternal success.

## 15.6 The Role of Good Deeds and Acts of Worship

Islam emphasizes performing good deeds and acts of worship to prepare for the Hereafter. These deeds range from obligatory acts like the five daily prayers, fasting in Ramadan, giving zakat (charity), and performing Hajj (pilgrimage), to voluntary acts like additional prayers, helping those in need, and spreading knowledge.

The Prophet Muhammad (peace and blessings be upon him) said: "Every Muslim has to give in charity." The people asked, "O Allah's Messenger! If someone has nothing to give, what will he do?" He said, "He should work with his hands and benefit himself and also give in charity (from what he earns)." The people further asked, "If he cannot do even that?" He replied, "He should help the needy who appeal for help." Then the people asked, "If he cannot do that?" He replied, "Then he should perform good deeds and keep away from evil deeds, and this will be regarded as charitable deeds." (Sahih Bukhari)

This hadith highlights the diverse forms of charity and good deeds, showing that every believer has an opportunity to earn rewards, regardless of their circumstances.

The belief in the Hereafter transforms a Muslim's approach to life, guiding them to live with purpose, accountability, and a constant awareness of the divine. It encourages self-reflection, repentance, and a commitment to align one's actions with Islamic principles. By embracing this belief, Muslims are motivated to lead lives filled with good deeds, compassion, and a deep connection with Allah, ultimately preparing for a successful journey in eternal life.

As we conclude this chapter, remember that the path to the Hereafter is paved with intentions and actions. Whether through prayer, charity, or simply being kind to others, every moment offers an opportunity to draw closer to Allah and prepare for the ultimate meeting with Him.

# Chapter Sixteen

# How Islam Transformed the Early Generation of Muslims

Islam's arrival in 7th-century Arabia brought about a profound transformation among its early followers. The early generation of Muslims, often referred to as the *Sahabah* (companions of the Prophet Muhammad, peace and blessings be upon him), experienced a significant shift in their worldview, ethics, and daily practices. This transformation was not merely spiritual but also social, economic, and political. Islam dramatically changed the lives of the early Muslims, setting a foundation for a new, just, and compassionate society.

## 16.1 Spiritual Awakening and Monotheism

Before the advent of Islam, the Arabian Peninsula was a land of polytheism and idol worship, with various tribes worshiping multiple gods and deities. The arrival of Islam, with its core message of Tawheed (the Oneness of God), brought a radical shift in the spiritual landscape, replacing the multitude of deities with a belief in one God, Allah. This belief instilled a sense of purpose, direction, and inner peace, replacing superstition and fear with faith and trust in a singular, compassionate Creator.

The concept of *Tawheed* redefined the relationship between the individual and the divine and between individuals themselves. It fostered a sense of equality and brotherhood among Muslims, transcending tribal and ethnic divisions. As the Qur'an states: "O mankind, We have created you from a male and a female, and made you into nations and tribes, so that you may know one another. Verily, the most honorable of you with Allah is the most righteous of you." (Qur'an, Al-Hujurat 49:13)

This verse emphasizes that in the eyes of Allah, all human beings are equal, and the only distinguishing factor is one's piety and righteousness.

## 16.2 Moral and Ethical Transformation

Islam introduced a comprehensive moral and ethical framework guiding early Muslims' daily lives. The teachings of the Qur'an and the Prophet Muhammad (peace be upon him) emphasized virtues such as honesty, justice, compassion, humility, and patience. These teachings profoundly impacted the early Muslims, transforming their conduct and social interactions.

The Prophet Muhammad (peace be upon him) is reported to have said: "I have been sent to perfect good character." (Musnad Ahmad). His teachings and personal example played a significant role in shaping early Muslims' moral and ethical framework.

The emphasis on good character and moral integrity led the early Muslims to abandon practices such as lying, cheating, and usury, which were prevalent in pre-Islamic Arabian society. Prohibiting interest (riba) and promoting fair trade practices helped create a just economic system that discouraged exploitation and promoted social welfare.

## 16.3 Social Justice and Community Building

One of the most significant transformations brought about by Islam was the emphasis on social justice and community welfare. Islam advocated for the rights of the marginalized, including orphans, widows, the poor, and slaves. The early Muslims were encouraged to support those in need, share their wealth, and foster a sense of solidarity and mutual aid.

The institution of *Zakat* (obligatory charity) was a revolutionary social welfare system that required Muslims to give a portion of their wealth to those less fortunate. This system helped redistribute wealth and reduce economic inequality, creating a more just and compassionate society.

The Qur'an states: "And establish prayer and give Zakat, and whatever good you put forward for yourselves – you will find it with Allah." (Qur'an, Al-Baqarah 2:110)

Additionally, Islam abolished many pre-Islamic practices that were unjust, such as female infanticide, and elevated the status of women by granting them rights to inheritance, education, and participation in social and political life. The Prophet Muhammad (peace be upon him) emphasized the importance of treating women with kindness and respect, stating: "The best of you are those who are best to their wives." (Tirmidhi)

## 16.4 Unity and Brotherhood

The early generation of Muslims experienced a profound sense of unity and brotherhood. The Qur'an and the teachings of the Prophet (peace and blessings be upon him) emphasized the importance of unity among Muslims, regardless of their tribal or ethnic backgrounds. This was a stark contrast to the tribalism and frequent inter-tribal conflicts that characterized pre-Islamic Arabia.

The concept of the *Ummah* (community of believers) united Muslims under a common faith, creating a strong sense of brotherhood and solidarity. The Prophet Muhammad (peace be upon him) reinforced this unity by establishing bonds of brotherhood between the *Muhajirun* (emigrants from Mecca) and the *Ansar* (helpers from Medina), setting an example of cooperation, mutual support, and love.

The Qur'an emphasizes this unity: "And hold firmly to the rope of Allah all together and do not become divided." (Qur'an, AleImran 3:103)

This unity was spiritual and practical, as the early Muslims came together to build a cohesive society based on justice, compassion, and mutual support.

## 16.5 Intellectual and Educational Transformation

Islam greatly encouraged the pursuit of knowledge and learning, transforming the early Muslims into a community that highly valued intellectual growth and education. The first revelation to the Prophet Muhammad (peace be upon him) began with the command to "Read" (Iqra), highlighting the importance of knowledge from the outset: "Read in the name of your Lord who created." (Qur'an, Al-Alaq 96:1)

The emphasis on knowledge led to a flourishing of intellectual activity among the early Muslims. They studied religious sciences and fields such as astronomy, medicine, mathematics, and philosophy. This quest for knowledge laid the groundwork for the later Islamic Golden Age, during which Islamic civilization made significant contributions to world knowledge.

The Prophet Muhammad (peace be upon him) said: "Seeking knowledge is an obligation upon every Muslim." (Ibn Majah)

This hadith underscored the importance of education for all Muslims, regardless of gender, encouraging both men and women to seek knowledge and understanding.

## 16.6 Political and Economic Reformation

The early Muslims were also transformed politically and economically through the principles and laws established by Islam. Establishing the Constitution of Madinah by the Prophet Muhammad (peace and blessings be upon him) was one of the earliest examples of a formal social contract that guaranteed religious freedom, protection of life and property, and mutual defense among Muslims and non-Muslims alike.

Islamic economic principles, such as the prohibition of usury (riba), the encouragement of trade and commerce, and the fair treatment of workers, led to a more just and equitable economic system. The emphasis on lawful (halal) earnings and wealth distribution through Zakat fostered a culture of ethical business practices and economic justice.

The early Muslims adopted these principles, transforming their society from one based on exploitation and tribal warfare to one characterized by justice, fairness, and social welfare.

## 16.7 Endurance and Resilience in Faith

Islam also instilled a profound sense of resilience and endurance in the early Muslims. Faced with persecution, hardship, and adversity, the early Muslims drew strength from their faith. The trials they endured, particularly during the early years in Mecca, forged a community of believers who were steadfast, patient, and unwavering in their commitment to their faith.

The Qur'an often speaks of the virtues of patience and perseverance: "O you who have believed, seek help through patience and prayer. Indeed, Allah is with the patient." (Qur'an, Al-Baqarah 2:153)

This verse and others like it were sources of comfort and encouragement for the early Muslims, helping them to remain steadfast in the face of adversity and to continue striving for the cause of Islam.

The transformation of the early generation of Muslims was comprehensive and multifaceted, touching every aspect of their lives—spiritual, moral, social, intellectual, political, and economic. The teachings of Islam provided a new worldview, one that was centered on the Oneness of God, ethical conduct, social justice, and intellectual growth. Through these teachings, the early Muslims built a cohesive, just, and thriving society that laid the foundation for the spread of Islam and its enduring legacy.

The transformation experienced by the early Muslims is an inspiring example of how faith when sincerely embraced and practiced, can lead to profound personal and societal change. It also reminds us of Islam's potential to guide individuals and communities toward a life of purpose, integrity, and fulfillment in both this world and the Hereafter.

# Chapter Seventeen
# The Islamic Golden Age and Lessons

The Islamic Golden Age, a period of cultural, economic, and scientific flourishing from the 8th to the 14th century, was a testament to the human spirit of inquiry and innovation. This era saw unprecedented advancements in science, medicine, mathematics, astronomy, literature, philosophy, and art. It was marked by the emergence of scholars and polymaths who, driven by their insatiable curiosity, made significant contributions that laid the foundation for modern science and knowledge. The Islamic Golden Age is often celebrated for its intellectual curiosity, where Islamic civilization absorbed and expanded upon the knowledge of previous civilizations, such as the Greeks, Persians, Indians, and Romans.

## 17.1 The House of Wisdom and the Translation Movement

One of the most iconic institutions of the Islamic Golden Age was the *House of Wisdom* ("Bayt al-Hikmah") in Baghdad. Established by Caliph Harun al-Rashid and later expanded by his son Al-Ma'mun in the early 9th century, the House of Wisdom was not just a building but a vibrant intellectual hub. Scholars from diverse backgrounds, with their unique perspectives and knowledge, gathered to study, translate, and expand upon the knowledge of ancient civilizations.

The *Translation Movement* was a crucial aspect of the Islamic Golden Age. It was not just about translating important works of Greek, Persian, and Indian origin into Arabic but about preserving and expanding knowledge through cross-cultural exchange. These translations, often accompanied by commentaries and expansions, allowed scholars to build upon the ideas and theories of earlier civilizations, demonstrating the importance of diversity and collaboration in intellectual progress.

Prominent translators such as Hunayn ibn Ishaq, a Christian Arab scholar, played a crucial role in preserving and enhancing the knowledge of earlier civilizations. He translated the works of Galen and Hippocrates into Arabic, thus ensuring the continuity of medical knowledge. This movement, which also included translating works in other fields, laid the groundwork for a culture of intellectual inquiry and scientific experimentation that characterized the Islamic Golden Age.

## 17.2 Advancements in Science and Medicine

The Islamic Golden Age is particularly renowned for its advancements in science and medicine. Muslim scholars approached these fields with a rigorous scientific method, emphasizing observation, experimentation, and compiling empirical data.

### Medicine

Islamic medicine, heavily influenced by earlier Greek and Indian texts, was significantly advanced by scholars such as Ibn Sina (Avicenna), whose work "The Canon of Medicine" (Al-Qanun fi al-Tibb) became a standard medical text in both the Islamic world and medieval Europe. Ibn Sina compiled a comprehensive medical encyclopedia that covered a wide range of topics, from anatomy and pharmacology to surgery and epidemiology. His approach combined clinical observations with theoretical insights, laying the foundation for modern medicine.

## Astronomy

Islamic astronomers made significant contributions to the field of astronomy. Al-Battani (Albategnius) refined the measurement of the solar year and developed trigonometric calculations that were crucial for later astronomical studies. Al-Zarqali (Arzachel) created accurate astronomical tables and was known for his work on the astrolabe. This instrument became essential for navigation and astronomy. Observatories, such as those in Baghdad and later in Maragheh, were established to study the stars and planets, leading to advancements in understanding celestial phenomena.

## Mathematics

Muslim mathematicians made groundbreaking contributions, particularly in algebra and geometry. Al-Khwarizmi, often called the "father of algebra," wrote "The Compendious Book on Calculation by Completion and Balancing" (Kitab al-Jabr wa-l-Muqabala), from which the term "algebra" is derived. His work laid the foundation for systematic solutions of linear and quadratic equations. Muslim mathematicians also played a crucial role in developing the Arabic numeral system, which included the concept of zero, borrowed from Indian mathematics. This system revolutionized mathematics and computation in the Islamic world and later Europe.

## 17.3 Contributions to Philosophy and Theology

The Islamic Golden Age was also a profound period of philosophical and theological exploration. Muslim scholars engaged with Greek philosophy, particularly the works of Plato and Aristotle, and sought to harmonize them with Islamic thought. This engagement gave rise to various schools of Islamic philosophy, such as Peripatetic (inspired by Aristotle) and Neoplatonism.

Al-Farabi, the "Second Teacher" (after Aristotle), was pivotal in integrating Greek philosophical traditions into Islamic thought. He wrote extensively on metaphysics, ethics, and political philosophy, influencing Islamic and Western philosophical traditions.

Ibn Rushd (Averroes), a prominent philosopher from Al-Andalus (Spain), is known for his commentaries on Aristotle. He sought to reconcile Aristotelian philosophy with Islamic theology, arguing that reason and revelation were compatible. His works profoundly influenced Muslim and Christian scholastic traditions, particularly in medieval Europe, where he was known as "The Commentator."

Al-Ghazali, a theologian and philosopher, is best known for his work "The Incoherence of the Philosophers" (Tahafut al-Falasifah), in which he critiqued the philosophical approach of earlier scholars, arguing that certain metaphysical concepts were beyond human reason and could only be understood through divine revelation. His works laid the foundation for Sufism (Islamic mysticism) and shaped Sunni Islamic thought.

## 17.4 Literature and the Arts

The Islamic Golden Age also saw a flourishing of literature and the arts. Muslim artists' and writers' creativity and innovation enriched poetry, prose, calligraphy, architecture, and visual arts.

### Literature

The period produced some of the greatest works of Arabic literature, including "One Thousand and One Nights" (Arabian Nights), a collection of stories that includes folk tales, fairy tales, and legends from across the Islamic world. Al-Mutanabbi, one of the greatest Arab poets, composed poetry that is still celebrated for its linguistic beauty and depth of meaning. Rumi, a Persian poet and Sufi mystic, wrote "The Masnavi," a poetic epic that continues to inspire readers worldwide with its spiritual insights and poetic elegance.

## Architecture and Calligraphy

Islamic art and architecture were also transformed during the Golden Age. Using geometric patterns, arabesques, and intricate calligraphy became hallmarks of Islamic artistic expression. Mosques, madrasas (educational institutions), and palaces were adorned with beautiful mosaics, tile work, and carvings that reflected Islam's spiritual and cultural ethos. The Great Mosque of Cordoba, the Alhambra in Granada, and the Dome of the Rock in Jerusalem are just a few examples of the architectural marvels from this period.

## 17.5 Impact on the Western World and Legacy

The Islamic Golden Age profoundly impacted the Western world, particularly during the European Renaissance. Many works of Muslim scholars were translated into Latin and studied in European universities. The knowledge preserved and expanded by Muslim scholars in fields such as medicine, mathematics, astronomy, and philosophy was crucial in shaping the intellectual landscape of medieval Europe.

Cordoba and Toledo in Spain became centers of learning where Muslim, Christian, and Jewish scholars interacted and exchanged ideas, further fostering cultural and intellectual exchange. The translation of works by Muslim scholars into Latin through the efforts of scholars like Gerard of Cremona introduced European scholars to new ideas in science, medicine, and philosophy.

The legacy of the Islamic Golden Age is evident today in numerous fields. Modern medicine, mathematics, science, and philosophy owe a great deal to the scholars of the Islamic Golden Age who preserved, enhanced, and transmitted the knowledge of ancient civilizations while contributing their own innovative ideas and discoveries.

The Islamic Golden Age was a period of remarkable cultural and intellectual achievement that left an indelible mark on the history of human civilization. It was characterized by a spirit of inquiry, a pursuit of knowledge, and a commitment to intellectual and cultural synthesis. The contributions made during this period continue to influence and inspire scholars and thinkers worldwide, serving as a testament to the transformative power of knowledge and the enduring legacy of Islamic civilization.

## 17.6 Lessons from the Islamic Golden Age

Muslims, as individuals, can learn invaluable lessons from the Islamic Golden Age by reflecting on the virtues that contributed to a thriving period of knowledge, culture, and spirituality. This era, characterized by remarkable advancements in science, medicine, mathematics, philosophy, and the arts, highlights the importance of seeking knowledge not just as an intellectual pursuit but as an act of worship and a means of positively impacting society. It emphasizes the value of intellectual curiosity, critical thinking, and striving for excellence in all areas of life. Moreover, the Islamic Golden Age demonstrates the importance of balancing worldly achievements with spiritual growth, reminding Muslims that their pursuit of knowledge should be guided by ethical principles and a commitment to serving humanity. Reflecting on the achievements of scholars who seamlessly integrated faith with reason inspires Muslims to adopt a mindset of lifelong learning, encourage cross-cultural and interdisciplinary collaboration, and make meaningful contributions in their lives, continuing the legacy of this extraordinary period in Islamic history.

By applying the lessons from the Islamic Golden Age, Muslims can transform themselves through the principles of knowledge, discipline, and ethical conduct in their everyday lives. First, by embracing the pursuit of knowledge, as demonstrated by the scholars of this era, Muslims can dedicate themselves to lifelong learning through formal education, self-study, or reflection on religious texts such as the Qur'an and Hadith. This ongoing quest for knowledge fosters personal growth and empowers them to contribute positively to society. Second, Muslims can achieve a balanced approach to life by integrating spiritual duties with personal and professional aspirations, ensuring their actions align with Islamic values and a commitment to justice and compassion. This balance allows them to excel in their careers while maintaining a strong spiritual foundation. Finally, by fostering cooperation and respect for diverse viewpoints,

Muslims can build more inclusive and harmonious communities, drawing inspiration from the Islamic Golden Age's example of cultural and intellectual exchange. By embodying these lessons, Muslims can become well-rounded individuals—spiritually grounded, intellectually enriched, ethically driven, and socially responsible—contributing to advancing their communities and the wider world.

# Chapter Eighteen

# Islamic Andalusian Age and Lessons from the Fall of Andalus

The Islamic Andalusian Age, often called *Al-Andalus*, represents a period of remarkable cultural, scientific, and intellectual flourishing in the Iberian Peninsula under Muslim rule. From the 8th to the 15th century, Islamic Spain was a beacon of knowledge, tolerance, and artistic expression. This era is celebrated for its achievements in various fields, including science, medicine, philosophy, architecture, literature, and interfaith harmony. It was a time when Muslims, Christians, and Jews coexisted and contributed to a rich and vibrant civilization that left a lasting legacy on both the Islamic world and Europe.

## 18.1 The Rise of Al-Andalus

The Islamic presence in the Iberian Peninsula began in 711 CE when an Umayyad Muslim army, led by Tariq ibn Ziyad, crossed the Strait of Gibraltar and defeated the Visigothic King Roderic. The swift Muslim conquest, characterized by relatively minimal bloodshed, established Islamic rule over much of the Iberian Peninsula. By 756 CE, Abd al-Rahman I, a member of the Umayyad dynasty who had escaped the Abbasid overthrow in Damascus, established an independent emirate in Cordoba, marking the beginning of the Umayyad Caliphate of Cordoba (929–1031 CE).

Under the Umayyads, Al-Andalus became a center of political stability, economic prosperity, and cultural vibrancy. The capital, Cordoba, emerged as one of the greatest cities of the medieval world, renowned for its impressive architecture, libraries, and institutions of learning. At its height, Al-Andalus stretched across much of present-day Spain and Portugal, serving as a model of Islamic governance and cultural excellence.

## 18.2 Cultural and Intellectual Achievements

The Islamic Andalusian Age is particularly noted for its cultural and intellectual achievements. Al-Andalus was a vibrant melting pot of diverse cultures, where knowledge from the Islamic world, classical antiquity, and other civilizations converged and thrived, creating a rich and fascinating history.

### Science and Medicine

Al-Andalus was not just a melting pot of cultures but also a hub for scientific inquiry and innovation. Scholars such as Ibn al-Nafis and Al-Zahrawi (known in the West as Abulcasis) made groundbreaking contributions to medicine and surgery, inspiring generations of scientists. Al-Zahrawi's Al-Tasrif, a comprehensive medical encyclopedia, influenced medical practice in the Islamic world and Europe for centuries. His works on surgical instruments and techniques laid the foundation for modern surgery.

### Philosophy and Theology

Andalusian scholars were instrumental in the transmission and development of philosophical thought. Ibn Rushd (Averroes), a renowned philosopher from Cordoba, is known for his commentaries on Aristotle, which significantly influenced Islamic and Western Christian philosophy. His works sparked a renewed interest in Aristotelian philosophy in Europe, particularly during the Scholastic period. Ibn Tufail and Ibn Bajja (Avempace) were key figures whose works explored the relationship between philosophy and religion.

## Mathematics and Astronomy

Andalusian scholars made significant advancements in mathematics and astronomy. Maslama al-Majriti contributed to the development of algebra and trigonometry. At the same time, Al-Zarqali (Arzachel) developed sophisticated astronomical tables and improved the design of the astrolabe, a critical instrument for celestial navigation. The Toledo School of Translators, a key institution in Al-Andalus, was pivotal in translating and disseminating Arabic scientific works to Europe, laying the groundwork for the Renaissance. Their translations of works by Andalusian scholars like Al-Zahrawi and Al-Majriti, among others, played a crucial role in the intellectual revival of Europe.

## Literature and Poetry

Al-Andalus was also a center of literary excellence. The era produced celebrated poets like Ibn Zaydun and Wallada bint al-Mustakfi, whose love poems are still cherished today. Ibn Hazm's The Ring of the Dove (Tawq al-Hamamah) is considered one of the most important works on love and human emotions, blending prose and poetry with philosophical insights. The literature of Al-Andalus was characterized by its sophistication, lyrical beauty, and exploration of themes ranging from love and politics to theology and ethics.

## 18.3 Architectural Marvels

Islamic architecture in Al-Andalus is renowned for its grandeur, intricacy, and innovative design. It combined elements from the Islamic world with local Andalusian traditions, resulting in a unique and stunning architectural style that has influenced subsequent architectural developments in both the Islamic world and Europe. The use of horseshoe arches, intricate tile work, and decorative stucco, all characteristic of Andalusian architecture, can be seen in many European buildings, particularly in Spain and Portugal, showcasing the enduring influence of Al-Andalus.

## The Great Mosque of Cordoba

Perhaps Islamic Spain's most iconic architectural achievement is the Great Mosque of Cordoba (La Mezquita). Initially built in 785 CE and expanded multiple times, the mosque is celebrated for its vast hypostyle hall with over 850 marble, granite, and jasper columns and distinctive horseshoe arches. The mosque also featured a mihrab (prayer niche) adorned with intricate mosaics and gold leaf, showcasing the artistic brilliance of Andalusian artisans. After the Reconquista, the mosque was converted into a cathedral, but much of its original Islamic architecture remains intact.

## The Alhambra Palace

Another masterpiece of Islamic architecture in Al-Andalus is the Alhambra in Granada. Built during the Nasrid dynasty (1238–1492 CE), the Alhambra is an exquisite palace and fortress complex renowned for its stunning Islamic calligraphy, detailed stucco work, and beautifully landscaped gardens with fountains and reflecting pools. With its harmonious blend of architecture, poetry, and nature, the Alhambra epitomizes Islamic art's aesthetic and spiritual ideals.

## The Alcazar of Seville

Originally a Moorish fort, the Alcazar of Seville was transformed into a royal palace that blends Islamic, Gothic, Renaissance, and Baroque architectural styles. Its Mudejar architecture, characterized by ornate tile work and intricate wood carvings, reflects the enduring influence of Islamic art and craftsmanship in post-Islamic Spain.

## 18.4 Religious Tolerance and Coexistence

One of the hallmarks of the Islamic Andalusian Age was the relative religious tolerance and coexistence among Muslims, Christians, and Jews. While not without its challenges, Al-Andalus was known for its *Convivencia*—a period of coexistence where diverse religious communities lived together, contributing to a rich and diverse cultural landscape.

## Jewish and Christian Communities

Under Islamic rule, Christians and Jews were granted protected status as *dhimmis* (protected non-Muslims). They were allowed to practice their religions, maintain their places of worship, and manage their communal affairs in exchange for a special tax (jizya). This relative tolerance allowed for a vibrant cultural and intellectual exchange among the three Abrahamic faiths. Jewish scholars like Maimonides (Rabbi Moses ben Maimon) flourished in Al-Andalus, contributing significantly to philosophy, medicine, and law. His works, such as the 'Guide for the Perplexed ', are still influential today. Similarly, Christian scholars and monks participated in the translation of Arabic scientific and philosophical texts into Latin, helping to transfer this knowledge to the rest of Europe. Their contributions to the translation movement in Al-Andalus were instrumental in the intellectual revival of Europe.

## Centers of Learning and Translation

Al-Andalus was home to numerous libraries and centers of learning, such as those in Cordoba, Toledo, and Granada. These centers became hubs for exchanging ideas and knowledge among Muslim, Christian, and Jewish scholars. The Toledo School of Translators, in particular, played a pivotal role in translating Arabic works into Latin, thereby preserving and transmitting classical knowledge to medieval Europe and fueling the Renaissance.

## 18.5 The Decline of Al-Andalus

The decline of Islamic rule in Spain began in the 11th century with internal strife and external pressures. The fall of the Umayyad Caliphate of Cordoba led to the fragmentation of Al-Andalus into smaller, rival kingdoms known as the *Taifas*. These divisions weakened Muslim rule, making it easier for northern

Christian kingdoms to reconquer territory gradually in a process known as the Reconquista.

Despite the efforts of later Muslim dynasties, such as the Almoravids and the Almohads, to defend Al-Andalus, the Christian reconquest continued. The last Muslim stronghold, the Kingdom of Granada, fell to the Catholic Monarchs Ferdinand and Isabella in 1492, marking the end of nearly eight centuries of Islamic rule in Spain.

The fall of Granada and the subsequent forced conversions, expulsions, and persecution of Muslims and Jews ended the era of relative tolerance and cultural flourishing that characterized much of the Andalusian age. Despite this, the legacy of Al-Andalus endures in the cultural, architectural, and intellectual heritage it left behind.

## 18.6 Legacy and Impact of the Andalusian Age

The Islamic Andalusian Age left an indelible mark on world history and culture. The intellectual, scientific, and artistic achievements of Al-Andalus contributed significantly to the European Renaissance. They laid the foundations for modern science, philosophy, and art.

### Influence on the Renaissance

Translating Arabic scientific, medical, and philosophical texts into Latin during the Middle Ages was crucial in Europe's intellectual awakening. The works of Ibn Rushd and other Andalusian philosophers heavily influenced scholars such as Thomas Aquinas. The transfer of knowledge from Al-Andalus to Europe through centers like Toledo helped catalyze the Renaissance, a renewed interest in classical knowledge and humanism.

### Cultural and Architectural Heritage

The architectural and artistic legacy of Al-Andalus continues to influence Spanish culture today. The Alhambra, the Great Mosque of Cordoba, and the Alcazar of Seville are UNESCO World Heritage sites and stand as testaments to Islamic Spain's artistic and cultural achievements. The enduring influence of Islamic art, architecture, and music can be seen in various elements of Spanish culture, including the famous Mudejar style that blends Islamic and Christian.

## 18.7 Lessons from Al Andalus

Muslims can use the lessons from the rise and fall of Al-Andalus to transform themselves by fostering unity, practicing steadfastness in their faith, and maintaining a commitment to knowledge and ethical conduct. The rise of Al-Andalus was marked by a spirit of inclusivity, intellectual pursuit, and adherence to Islamic principles, which led to the flourishing of culture, science, and society. Muslims can learn from this by striving to create environments in their personal and communal lives that encourage learning, collaboration, and mutual respect, regardless of cultural or religious differences. Embracing the value of knowledge and wisdom to serve faith and community can lead to personal growth and societal progress.

Conversely, the fall of Al-Andalus serves as a powerful reminder of the dangers of disunity, internal strife, and deviation from core Islamic values. Muslims can take this as a lesson in maintaining solidarity and working together towards common goals, avoiding the pitfalls of division and discord. By staying vigilant against complacency, remaining firm in their religious duties, and promoting justice and moral integrity, Muslims can avoid the mistakes that led to the decline of Al-Andalus. By integrating these lessons into their daily lives, Muslims can become more resilient, united, and ethically driven individuals, better prepared to face modern challenges while upholding their faith and contributing positively to society.

# Conclusion

As we reach the end of this book, *Islamic Transformation*, we must reflect on our journey through its pages. This book explored how embracing Islamic teachings can profoundly transform various aspects of an individual's life, from spiritual growth to personal development, ethical behavior to social engagement, and managing worldly affairs to preparing for the Hereafter. Each chapter has highlighted how the principles of Islam offer a comprehensive framework for achieving inner peace, fulfillment, and a deeper connection with the Divine.

Islam is not just a religion but a complete way of life that addresses the needs of the human soul, mind, and body. It provides guidance on how to lead a meaningful and purpose-driven life while emphasizing the importance of moral integrity, community service, and personal accountability.

## Embracing Transformation in Everyday Life

The transformation that Islam offers begins with an inner awakening—a conscious realization of the need to align one's life with divine guidance. This awakening is often sparked by a personal experience, a profound question about life's purpose, or a desire for inner peace and fulfillment. Whatever the trigger, the journey toward transformation requires sincerity, commitment, and an open heart.

In practical terms, embracing transformation means taking small, consistent steps toward self-improvement. It involves setting aside time for daily prayers, engaging in regular self-reflection, seeking knowledge, and practicing gratitude. It means striving to be kind, just, and compassionate in all interactions, recognizing that every action has both worldly and spiritual significance.

Muslims are encouraged to see their lives as a constant journey toward self-betterment, where every moment offers an opportunity to grow closer to Allah. This journey is marked by striving (jihad) to overcome one's lower desires and weaknesses and continuously working to embody the values of patience, humility, generosity, and forgiveness.

## A Call to Action: Inviting Readers to Explore Further

This book aims to inspire readers to explore the transformative power of Islam further. Whether you are a Muslim seeking to deepen your faith or a non-Muslim curious about Islamic teachings, I invite you to approach this exploration with an open mind and heart. Reflect on the concepts discussed and consider how they might apply to your own life. Islam offers a wealth of wisdom and guidance relevant to people of all backgrounds and walks of life.

For Muslims, this journey is a call to renew their intentions and strive for excellence in their worship, character, and conduct. It reminds them to prioritize the Hereafter over the temporary pleasures of this world and to engage in acts of worship and good deeds with sincerity and devotion.

This book offers non-Muslims a glimpse into how Islamic teachings can bring about meaningful transformation. It encourages readers to look beyond common stereotypes and misconceptions and explore Islam as a source of spiritual enrichment and ethical guidance.

## Finding Strength in Faith

One of the most profound aspects of Islam is its emphasis on finding strength and comfort in faith. Islam teaches that every challenge, hardship, and joy is part of a divine plan to bring believers closer to Allah. This belief fosters resilience, patience, and a positive outlook, even in adversity.

In times of difficulty, Muslims are reminded to turn to Allah for guidance and support, to maintain trust in His wisdom, and to remember that every trial is an opportunity for growth and purification. This faith-based resilience is a transformative force, enabling individuals to navigate life's ups and downs with grace and steadfastness.

The Qur'an beautifully captures this sentiment: "So verily, with the hardship, there is relief. Verily, with the hardship, there is relief." (Qur'an 94:5-6)

These ayahs remind believers that no matter how challenging life may become, there is always ease and relief that follows. This assurance provides comfort and hope, encouraging a mindset that sees beyond the immediate difficulties to the rewards and blessings that lie ahead.

## The Promise of the Hereafter

As discussed in the final chapter, the belief in the Hereafter is a cornerstone of the Islamic faith that profoundly influences a Muslim's outlook on life. This belief instills a sense of purpose, accountability, and hope, motivating believers to live in a manner that pleases Allah and prepares them for eternal success.

Understanding that every action, no matter how small, has consequences in the Hereafter encourages Muslims to strive for excellence in all aspects of their lives. It fosters a mindset that values both spiritual and material pursuits, balancing worldly ambitions with achieving Allah's pleasure and attaining Paradise.

## The Path Forward

The path to transformation through Islam is an ongoing journey of learning, reflection, and action. It requires sincerity, dedication, and a willingness to grow and change. While the path may sometimes be challenging, the rewards—both in this world and the Hereafter—are immense.

As you move forward, consider the following steps to continue your journey toward transformation:

1. Deepen Your Understanding: Continue to seek knowledge about Islam and its teachings. Read the Qur'an with reflection, study the life of the Prophet Muhammad (peace be upon him), and engage with Islamic scholars and communities.

2. Reflect on Your Actions: Regularly assess your actions, intentions, and behaviors. Are they aligned with Islamic teachings? Are there areas where you can improve or grow?

3. Engage in Worship and Good Deeds: Make worship a central part of your daily routine. Engage in acts of charity, kindness, and service to others. Remember that every good deed is a step toward spiritual growth, no matter how small.

4. Build a Supportive Community: Surround yourself with people who inspire and support your journey of faith. Engage with your local mosque, participate in Islamic events, and build relationships with others who share your values and aspirations.

5. Stay Resilient and Hopeful: Life is full of ups and downs, but Islam teaches that every hardship is an opportunity for growth. Stay resilient, maintain your faith, and always trust in Allah's wisdom and mercy.

## A Journey of Continuous Growth

Ultimately, the transformation that Islam offers is a journey of continuous growth and self-improvement. It is a path that calls for sincerity, commitment, and a deep desire to live a pleasing life to Allah. As you embark on or continue this journey, remember that you are never alone—Allah is always with you, guiding, supporting, and providing for you every step.

***Islamic Transformation*** is an invitation to embark on a lifelong journey of growth, grounded in the wisdom of small, consistent changes. By cultivating habits rooted in faith and sincerity, you can nurture a deeper relationship with Allah, enrich your character, and bring a sense of purpose and fulfillment into your everyday life. Transformation does not happen overnight; it is a gentle evolution shaped by persistence, patience, and trust in Allah's plan.

This book is just the beginning. There is always more to learn, more to reflect on, and more ways to grow closer to Allah. May Allah guide us all on this path of transformation, fill our hearts with His light, and grant us success in this world and the Hereafter.

May your journey toward transformation through Islam be filled with enlightenment, peace, and fulfillment. Remember, every positive change, no matter how small, draws you closer to becoming the best version of yourself—a version that pleases Allah and serves as a beacon of goodness to those around you.

This concludes the book. May it serve as a source of inspiration, guidance, and encouragement on your path to personal and spiritual growth.

# End Book Review Request Page

Dear Reader,

Thank you for embarking on the journey of **Islamic Transformation**. Your support and feedback are truly invaluable. I hope this book has enriched your understanding and equipped you with the tools to improve your life. Now that you have everything needed to achieve your goals, it's time to share your newfound knowledge and guide others toward the same support.

Your honest review will help spread this message to a wider audience. Whether you choose to share your thoughts on Amazon, Goodreads, or any other platform, your feedback is deeply appreciated.

Please click the link or scan the QR code below to leave your review if you haven't done so earlier.

https://www.amazon.com/review/review-your-purchases/?asin=B0DJR1BGWT

Again, Thank you for your support and for participating in this journey. May Allah reward you and bless you and your family in this life and the next. Aameen.

Your Sister in Islam
Aisha Othman

# References

- Ahmad, I. (1999). Parenting in the West: An Islamic perspective. Amana Publications.

- Ahmed, S. (2016). *What is Islam? The importance of being Islamic.* Princeton University Press.

- Al-Bukhari, M. I. (1971). *Sahih al-Bukhari* (M. Muhsin Khan, Trans.). Darussalam Publishers.

- Al-Daffa, A. A. (1984). *The Muslim contribution to mathematics.* Croom Helm.

- Al-Ghazali, A. H. (2004). *Inner Dimensions of Islamic Worship.* Islamic Texts Society.

- Al-Ghazali, M. (1991). The Alchemy of Happiness (C. Field, Trans.). Maktaba Qasimul Uloom.

- Al-Ghazali, M. (2005). The Inner Dimensions of Islamic Worship. Islamic Book Trust.

- Armstrong, K. (2002). *Islam: A Short History.* Modern Library.

- Arnaldez, R. (2004). *Averroes: A Rationalist in Islam.* University of Notre Dame Press.

- Bloom, J., & Blair, S. (2009). *The Grove Encyclopedia of Islamic Art and

*Architecture*. Oxford University Press.

- Brown, J. A. C. (2014). *Misquoting Muhammad: The Challenge and choices of interpreting the Prophet's Legacy*.Oneworld Publications.

- Bukhari, M. I. I. (1971). Sahih Bukhari (M. Muhsin Khan,Trans.). Darussalam Publishers.

- Dodds, J. D., Menocal, M. R., & Balbale, A. K. (2008). *TheArts of Intimacy: Christians, Jews, and Muslims in the Making of Castilian Culture*. Yale University Press.

- Esposito, J. L. (2001). What Everyone Needs to Know About Islam. Oxford University Press.

- Fierro, M. (2005). *Andalusi Knowledge in the Mediterranean: Intellectual Networks in the Twelfth to Fourteenth Centuries*.Cambridge University Press.

- Fletcher, R. A. (2006). *Moorish Spain*. University of California Press.

- Gutas, D. (1998). *Greek Thought, Arabic Culture: The Graeco-Arabic Translation Movement in Baghdad and Early Abbasid Society(2nd-4th/8th-10th centuries)*. Routledge.

- Hassan, M. K. (2010). *The rise and fall of Islamic Science: The calendar as a case study*. American Journal of Islamic SocialSciences, 27(3), 78-97.

- Ibn Kathir, I. (2003). TafsirIbn Kathir (Abridged) (S.al-Mubarakpuri, Trans.). Darussalam Publishers.

- Ibn Majah, M. Y. (2007). Sunan Ibn Majah (N. A. Naser,Trans.). Dar Al Manarah.

- Ibn Sina (Avicenna). (1999). *The Canon of Medicine(Al-Qanun fi al-Tibb)*. (O. H. Karim, Trans.). Kazi Publications.

- Jasser Auda. *Maqasid al-Shariah as Philosophy of Islamic Law: A Systems Approach.*

- Kamali, M. H. (2002). *The Dignity of Man: An Islamic Perspective.* Islamic Texts Society.

- Kennedy, H. (1996). *Muslim Spain and Portugal: A Political History of al-Andalus.* Routledge.

- Khan, M. M., & Al-Hilali, T.M. (1996). Interpretation of the Meanings of The Noble Qur'an in the English Language. Dar-us-Salam Publications.

- Khan, M. M. (1997). The Translation of the Meanings of Sahih Al-Bukhari. Darussalam Publishers.

- Makdisi, G. (1981). *The Rise of Colleges: Institutions of Learning in Islam and the West.* Edinburgh University Press.

- Menocal, M. R. (2002). *The Ornament of the World: How Muslims, Jews, and Christians Created a Culture of Tolerance in Medieval Spain.* Little, Brown, and Company.

- Muslim, I. A. (1971). Sahih Muslim (A. Siddiqi, Trans.). Kitab Bhavan.

- Nadwi, A. H. (1993). Islam and the World: The Rise and Decline of Muslims and its Effect on Mankind. Academy of Islamic Research and Publications.

- Nasr, S. H. (2002). *The Heart of Islam: Enduring Values for Humanity.* Harper One.

- Nasr, S. H. (2006). *Islamic Philosophy from Its Origin to the Present: Philosophy in the Land of Prophecy.* State University of New York Press.

- Nasr, S. H. (2002). The Heart of Islam: Enduring Values for Humanity. HarperOne.

- Nasr, S. H. (Ed.). (2015). *The Study Quran: A New Translation and Commentary*. Harper One.

- Nawawi, Y. M. (1999). *Riyad-us-Saliheen.* . Dar-us-Salam Publications.

- Nawawi, I. (1999). *Riyadhas-Salihin (The Gardens of the Righteous)* (M. Z. Khan, Trans.). Dar AlTaqwa Ltd.

- O'Callaghan, J. F. (1983). *A History of Medieval Spain*. Cornell University Press.

- Qaradawi, Y. (1999). The Lawful and the Prohibited in Islam(A. Siddiqui, Trans.). American Trust Publications.

- Rabbani, F. (2017). Absolute Essentials of Islam: Faith, Prayer & the Path of Salvation According to the Hanafi School. Fons Vitae.

- Ramadan, T. (2004). Western Muslims and the Future of Islam. Oxford University Press.

- Ramadan, T. (2009). In the Footsteps of the Prophet: Lessons from the Life of Muhammad*. Oxford UniversityPress.

- Ruggles, D. F. (2000). *Gardens, Landscape, and Vision in the Palaces of Islamic Spain*. Penn State University Press.

- Safran, J. M. (2013). *The Second Umayyad Caliphate: The Articulation of Caliphal Legitimacy in al-Andalus*. Harvard UniversityPress.

- Saliba, G. (2007). *Islamic Science and the Making of the European Renaissance*. The MIT Press.

- Siddiqui, M. (1993). *Hadith Literature: Its Origin, Development, & Special Features*. Islamic Texts Society.

- Siddiqui, M. (1993). Hadith Literature: Its Origin, Development, & Special Features*. Islamic TextsSociety.

- Sivan, E. (1985). Radical Islam: Medieval Theology and Modern Politics. Yale University Press.

- Suleiman, O., & Elshinawy, M.(2019). *Prayers of the pious*. Kube Publishing Ltd.

- Sunnah.com (n.d.) Jami' At-Tirmidhi
  https://sunnah.com/tirmidhi

- Sunnah.com (n.d.) Musnad Ahmad
  https://sunnah.com/ahmad

- Sunnah.com (n.d.) Sahih al-Bukhari
  https://sunnah.com/bukhari

- Sunnah.com (n.d.) Sahih Muslim
  https://sunnah.com/muslim

- Sunnah.com (n.d.) Sunan Abi Dawud
  https://sunnah.com/abudawud

- Sunnah.com (n.d.) Sunan An-Nasa'i
  https://sunnah.com/nasai

- Sunnah.com (n.d.) Sunan Ibn Majah
  https://sunnah.com/ibnmajah

- Sunnah.com. (n.d.). *Riyad as-Salihin 1490 - The Book of Du'a (Supplications)*
  https://sunnah.com/riyadussalihin:1490

- The Quranic Arabic Corpus. (n.d.). Word-by-word grammar, syntax, and morphology of the Holy Quran.
  https://corpus.quran.com/wordmorphology.jsp

- Toomer, G. J. (1964). *Al-Khwarizmi, Abu Ja'far Muhammadibn Musa*. Dictionary of Scientific Biography, 7, 357-363.

- Toorawa, S. M. (2015). *Consistent living in Islam: Practices and principles*. The Islamic Foundation.

- Turner, H. (1997). *Science in Medieval Islam: An Illustrated Introduction*. University of Texas Press.

- Wadud, A. (2006). Inside the Gender Jihad: Women's Reform in Islam. Oneworld Publications.

- Watt, W. M. (1972). *The Influence of Islam on Medieval Europe*. Edinburgh University Press.

- Yusuf, H. (2004). *Purification of the Heart: Signs, Symptoms, and Cures of the Spiritual Diseases of the Heart*. StarlatchPress.

Made in the USA
Columbia, SC
03 November 2024